BRIDESMAID ON A BUDGET

BOOKS BY SHARON NAYLOR

The Bridesmaid Handbook

Your Special Wedding Toasts

The Ultimate Bridal Shower Idea Book

Love Bets: 300 Romantic Wagers to Up the Ante on your Love Life

Your Wedding, Your Way

The Bride's Diplomacy Guide

Renewing Your Wedding Vows

The Essential Guide to Wedding Etiquette

The Busy Bride's Essential Wedding Checklists

The Ultimate Wedding Registry Workbook

Your Special Wedding Vows

The Mother of the Bride Book

Mother of the Groom

The Groom's Guide

1000 Best Wedding Bargains

1000 Best Secrets for Your Perfect Wedding

How to Have a Fabulous Wedding for $10,000 or Less

The Complete Outdoor Wedding Planner

How to Plan an Elegant Wedding in 6 Months or Less

It's My Wedding Too: A Novel

Bridesmaid on a Budget

How to be a Brilliant Bridesmaid without Breaking the Bank

SHARON NAYLOR

SEAL PRESS

Bridesmaid on a Budget
How to Be a Brilliant Bridesmaid without Breaking the Bank

Copyright © 2011 by Sharon Naylor

44913795 1/11

Published by
Seal Press
A Member of the Perseus Books Group
1700 Fourth Street
Berkeley, California

Library of Congress Cataloging-in-Publication Data

Naylor, Sharon.
  Bridesmaid on a budget : how to be a brilliant bridesmaid without breaking the bank
/ Sharon Naylor.
    p. cm.
  ISBN 978-1-58005-337-2
  1. Bridesmaids. I. Title.
  BJ2065.W43N395 2011
  395.2'2–dc22

                                              2010023244 2010030224

9 8 7 6 5 4 3 2 1

Cover design by Domini Dragoone
Interior design by Megan Jones Design
Printed in the United States of America
Distributed by Publishers Group West

For my bridesmaids,
Jill, Jen, Pam, and Madison

Contents

Introduction

When you hear those words, *Will you be my bridesmaid?* from the newly engaged, radiant bride you love, *you* become pretty radiant yourself! It's so incredibly exciting to be asked into the bride's Inner Circle, to be named among the most important women in the world to her. Of all of the people she knows, she wants *you* to stand up with her as she takes her wedding vows and begins her new life. It's pretty fabulous to be named, and pretty fabulous to look ahead at all of the fun and glamour to come. Trying on designer gowns, planning a lavish and lovely bridal shower worthy of a photo feature in the top bridal magazines, throwing an unforgettable bachelorette bash, walking down the aisle with all eyes on you as the ceremony begins (and maybe you'll get the Hot Groomsman paired up with you!). This is where you have a lot in common with the bride: such dreamy, detailed plans to make, so many thrills in the months to come....

Well, maybe that's not your take on it. If you've been a bridesmaid before—perhaps many times before—you know that it's not always such a dreamy, effervescent time. After all, you know from experience that being a bridesmaid can sometimes mean dealing with a bride who transforms into a demanding drama queen, or *Mean Girls* antics from the other bridesmaids, and a list of "responsibilities" that grows every day. Right now, you might be more likely to down a margarita to calm your nerves than to

1

celebrate the "thrills of the months to come." Especially since you know what being a bridesmaid can *cost*.

No matter which end of the spectrum you fall on, here's the reality: Being a bridesmaid costs *money*. Lots of it. Sometimes, lots and lots of it. Just take a look at this chart from the wedding industry survey site TheWeddingReport.com to see the *national average expenses* of bridesmaids across the country:

> *Bridesmaid Market Overview: In 2009, bridesmaids will spend an estimated $9.61 billion. Results from our recent bridesmaid study concluded there are an average 4.3 bridesmaids per wedding accounting for an estimated 9.53 million bridesmaids spending $9.61 billion. A single bridesmaid will* **spend $1,069–$1,269 on dress to travel.**

The average number of times someone is a bridesmaid is **three, which translates to well over $3,000 spent by each bridesmaid in her life.**

- 10.93 percent of you have been a bridesmaid once (including now)

- 67.07 percent of you have been a bridesmaid between 2 and 5 times

- 14.90 percent of you have been a bridesmaid between 6 and 20 times

- 7.1 percent of you have been a bridesmaid *more than ten times*

THEWEDDINGREPORT.COM'S SURVEY RESULTS FOR 2009*

BACHELORETTE PARTY EXPENSES	$152
BRIDAL SHOWER GIFT	$72
BRIDAL SHOWER PLANS	$60 TO $200 PER BRIDESMAID
BRIDESMAID ACCESSORIES	$52
BRIDESMAID DRESS	$178
BRIDESMAID DRESS ALTERATIONS	$56
SHOES	$49
HAIR STYLING	$65
MANICURE (PLUS TIPS)	$32
PEDICURE	$30
OUTFIT FOR REHEARSAL DINNER	$71
PLANE FARE	$303
HOTEL (PER NIGHT)	$140
RENTAL CAR (PER DAY)	$88
WEDDING GIFT FROM BRIDESMAID	$117

*EVERY CATEGORY IS PROJECTED TO INCREASE MODERATELY IN EXPENSE BY 2014, ACCORDING TO SURVEYS CONDUCTED BY THEWEDDINGREPORT.COM.

And these are the *national average* figures, combining the sky-high prices of the Northeast with the more moderate prices of the South and the Midwest. If you're a southern woman, you might look at that $32 for a manicure figure and laugh in disbelief. If you're a New York City or Boston woman, $32 might get you very, very excited and Googling to see where you can get a manicure for that low price.

No matter how the individual expenses stack up per category for this wedding, you're looking at a cash outlay of about $1,000. More or less. And in this economy, with where you are in life—maybe just graduating college or still in school and eating Ramen noodles, recently married and buying your own first home, struggling to make ends meet in a frustrating and low-paying job that drives you crazy but you'd still hate to get laid off anytime soon—that's a lot of money to devote to anything.

"A thousand dollars? That's two rent payments," says one bridesmaid, whose bliss bubble has burst after a week of being named to a bridal party. "It's going to be tough to come up with that kind of cash."

"My boyfriend is already paying most of the bills in our apartment," says another bridesmaid. "He knows I've said yes to being in the bridal party, but I'm already anxious about each check I'm going to have to write for my friend's wedding."

And then there's, "There goes my ski trip!"

But of course, there's also this: "I know it's going to cost a lot, but the bride is so very important to me, and this is just a short time of stretching my dollars. So whatever she wants, I'll find a way."

Kinda want to smack this last one, don't you? That's the kind of breezy attitude tossed around by bridesmaids who aren't living from paycheck to paycheck, who have plenty of room on their credit cards, or who have parents who hand out cash like candy on Halloween. But the truth is, we *all* have that belief deep inside of us. We love the bride. We'd do anything for her. And we're trying to balance our money panic with a very real sense of, "It's worth it."

That's quite a seesaw, so get your Dramamine ready, because you're going to be swinging back and forth between the two—money terror and friendly benevolence—until the day you walk down the aisle ahead of her . . . and maybe for a few months afterward when the credit card bills start rolling in.

What you've got here, though, is a handbook of secrets that's going to cut down on your bridesmaid money terror. *Way* down. *Way, way* down. Because you get insider scoop on where to find fabulous bridesmaid's dresses for a fraction of the national average price. And expert advice on how to throw a stylish shower that only *looks* expensive, but really costs very little. And . . . get ready for it . . . the *power to have a say in what you'll be spending.*

That's right. Forget about that common misperception that the bride says what she wants and you whip out your wallet. You'll find out here how to get a strong say in what your expenses will be, no matter how big a Bridezilla you're dealing with. It's all in your timing and saying the right thing the right way at the right time. Pretty soon, the bride's on your side, welcoming your budget-friendly ideas, in the ultimate healthy relationship based on compromise and creativity.

You'll learn how to flex your budget muscles within the circle of bridesmaids, too, which can be a pretty scary place to be when you're the one with the money concerns and everyone else is ready to spend top dollar. Or if you have a control-freak Maid of Honor running wild with the plans and sending you emails of what you owe to cover your part of what she's gone ahead and planned. We've got that problem solved! You're going to find out how to thrive within the bridesmaid brigade, and probably be a dream come true to the rest of the budget-seeking bridesmaids, too.

You could probably count on one hand the number of bridesmaids who didn't have complaints about being pressured to spend more money than they wanted to . . . but they all walked their bridesmaid walk *before this book came out*. You're among the lucky ones, because there's now a money rescue book just for you. For the Brilliant Bridesmaid on a Budget.

You've got me as your guide and coach, and everything you pay half as much for is going to look like you spent three or four times the amount. I'm not sending you down the aisle in a crappy polyester dress—with giant butt bows and sequins—that they were giving away for $2 at an online auction, and I'm not going to let you plan a cheapo, cash bar, not-enough-food bridal shower that gets the gossips' tongues wagging. I'm looking out for you. Everything's going to be *beautiful*.

And you can take that to the bank. Along with all the money you have left from your monthly paycheck.

Ready to get started? Let's go. . . .

BEFORE YOU CLICK BUY

No shopping for you until you read this! You might be so used to your favorite websites, thinking they're the best deals around, that you don't even know there might be a better way. Happens to all of us. Happily and thankfully, the Internet gods have come to our rescue with some great price-comparison sites, some you might know about and some might be new to you. It works like this: Let's say you're shopping for a great pair of shoes, since the sweet and considerate bride has allowed all of the bridesmaids to choose their own strappy, silver heels. You love Cole Haan heels, so you're ready to find the best price out there.

Just type the particular style and size of Cole Haan heels (all in quotation marks, so that the site delivers just what you're looking for and not 10,000 other partial matches!) into the following shopper's delight sites, and they'll show you which online source has the best prices going right now:

- BizRate.com
- Dealtime.com
- NextTag.com
- PriceGrabber.com
- Shopping.com
- Shopping.Yahoo.com
- Shopzilla.com

Wait, where's eBay? eBay is still a fabulous place to find bargains, and maybe your shoes are up for auction there right now. But professional shoppers say that eBay's new turn toward Buy It Now rather than auctions is cutting down on your odds of finding Ferragamos for $10. So by all means, check eBay. But use these price-comparison sites to give you the best chances of the fabulous find.

Here's a tip for your eBay finds: Seasoned eBay shoppers say that you can win great bargains by jumping into auctions that end late at night *Pacific time*, when many East Coasters have gone to sleep. And of course, they warn to be very careful to shop from authenticated sellers, to check for brand authenticity, to not trust photographs solely, to message the sellers to ask questions about the products, to check out feedback ratings and comments to scout out rip-off artists, and to shop securely. Timing mixed with smart shopping can get you those Cole Haans or those Ferragamos for $8.

eBay's New Competitors

If eBay's evolution means there may be fewer steals on the auction block, a flock of newcomers are quick on their heels to fill the void. Here are some auction sites that could be your next favorite bargain-hunting home:

- Bonanzle.com (Look for their sale "bonanzas," during which sellers put everything they're selling on mega-sale.)

- Crater.com (Lots of Buy It Now, but you can make multiple purchases from different vendors with one checkout, unlike at eBay. So you can nab some savings faster.)

- OnlineAuction.com

YES, COUPONS ARE COOL

Before we get into each category of planning—and all the fabulous ways you can save—let me first do three cheers for coupons. And coupon *codes*, since so much of your shopping will be done online. If you think coupons are for grannies or for grocery shopping, then you can go ahead and pay full price while the rest of us get 15 percent, 20 percent, 25 percent or more off every purchase we make. How does 65 percent off sound? That's possible, too, with the right coupon at the right time at the right store.

Coupons *are* cool. And extremely smart for the budget-brilliant bridesmaid.

Throughout this book, I'll remind you to Google for coupons, or go to my favorite coupon websites where you'll find discounts at the top stores like Macy's, Bloomie's, and even at Target. But here's where I'll start your list so that you can *bookmark them on your computer*. Visit the following *free* coupon sites, and check back in twice a month to snag their new listings. Just be aware that smart shopping is always in order—don't sign on to paid coupon sites, and don't share any of your personal information anywhere. Those e-thieves are out there, quite clever in how they attempt to steal. I've used the following coupon sites to great effect, so here you go:

- CoolSavings.com
- CouponAlbum.com
- CouponGood.org
- Coupons.com
- CouponCabin.com
- CouponMom.com
- CouponMountain.com
- Dealio.com
- DealzConnection.com
- Extrabux.com
- FabulousSavings.com
- FatWallet.com
- RetailMeNot.com
- SavingPiggy.com
- SmartSource.com
- UltimateCoupons.com
- ValPak.com

Tweeting for Coupons

Several Twitter-based coupon sources have popped up recently, with more popping up every day, so check out Redtagtweets .com and CouponTweet.com, two sites that search all of Twitter to locate the kinds of coupons you need.

And then there are gift cards. Check out Plasticjungle.com to snag secondhand gift cards, which may have been traded in by someone who received a Victoria's Secret gift card for a birthday gift but doesn't wear lingerie or sweatpants with PINK written across the butt. These people trade their gift cards in to this site, they get some cash in return, and you get the $25 or $50 gift card for up to 40 percent off face value. The site is so big, it's attracted over 1,400 big-name retailers. Use that gift card to buy your dress from Nordstrom, or maybe give that $100 Bed Bath & Beyond gift card to the bride as her shower gift! She doesn't have to know you only paid $60 for it! Sweet savings.

And to close out our Day One session of savings-hunting, be aware that retailers go nuts with their coupons, freebie offers, and free shipping starting in October and going right through to January. So if it's that time of the year right now, even if the wedding is in late summer, it's never too early to shop for the bride and groom's gifts, or for the paper and craft supplies you'll need for shower invitations, favors, and other items. Just like the bride who's saving an impressive 50 percent to 75 percent on her wedding costs by planning her wedding in the smartest season with the biggest bargains, you're making the calendar work for you!

Part One

The Fun Begins

CHAPTER 1

Before Anyone Else Knows

*H*ere's one of the most surprising bridesmaid budget mistakes: spending too much on Day One to celebrate the bride and groom's great news.

The average excited bridesmaid—not fully aware of how much spending is to be done in the upcoming months—very sweetly and generously offers to host a celebration party. Good food, good friends, lots of wine and champagne—a mini-wedding, if you will! And when the party plans take off, it's very easy to overspend. By hundreds of dollars. "To do it right, we had to do it up," says one bridesmaid, who spent over $500 on catering and drinks for the party she hosted. "It was a blast, but I felt the debt impact immensely. It made it hard to budget for other purchases that came up quickly."

It's a wonderful idea to toast the upcoming nuptials and earn your stripes as a Dream Bridesmaid—and what bride wouldn't want a party with friends?—but there are other ways to celebrate that don't cost a fortune. Some cost *nothing*. Here are some alternative ways to start the bride's Big Wedding Season in style, or in sentimental ways, that still make her day:

• Dinner at your place. In place of the big group party, break out your favorite recipes and make a fabulous dinner for her and her groom. A relaxed couples' night may be the perfect start to your shared wedding planning experience, and isn't it better to spend $50 on all your menu prep and a bottle or two of wine than $500? Check out recipes at www.foodtv.com to get your favorite Food Network chefs' specialty recipes for inspiration, since making a meal means so much more to the bride because you invested time, effort, and ingenuity into the celebration.

• Get out in nature. This, too, can become your wedding planning season ritual, as you fulfill the bridesmaid role of listening to the bride, letting her talk about her ideas and feelings, wiping out wedding stress. Before the wedding plans get hectic, before her future mother-in-law starts to mess with the plans, you give the bride the gift of time alone with you out in beautiful scenery, which research shows is a natural stress-buster. And you rock as the bridesmaid who started it all. Now *that's* a good gift. And it costs nothing.

• Bring her to the family. If you've grown up together and she's like a second daughter to your parents, invite her to your parents' house and childhood home where you grew up and shared countless sleepovers and days by the pool. So many memories there! And a great time to reminisce and relax.

• Get a meaningful gift for her. It could be a pretty $5 journal from the bookstore, which you present to the bride for her to record what's going *well* with her wedding plans—a gratitude journal that will keep her balanced and will serve as a priceless keepsake. This is one of my favorite gifts for brides: a greeting card keepsake box. From now until the wedding day, she's going to receive tons of cards from her loved ones—engagement cards, bridal shower cards, wedding cards, love notes from her groom—and this collection is incredibly valuable. So with just a few dollars spent at the craft store, and maybe an hour of DIY time, you'll have a pretty box or lidded basket decorated with her favorite color of ribbon or pretty silk gardenias in which to store all of her cards. Your price: often under $10. And again, it's *priceless* to the bride.

And of course, one of the best ways to start the bride's wedding planning season, as well as your season in her bridal party, is to offer her your assistance in any way she needs, telling her never to be shy about asking

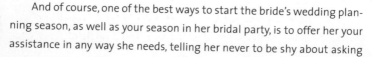

for your advice or help. Today's considerate brides—the ones who don't get featured on sensationalistic television shows—worry a lot about burdening their bridesmaids, so they hesitate to ask for their time and assistance. But when you say, "Call me anytime," that bride is going to be wildly happy.

THE BEST THING YOU CAN DO FOR YOUR BUDGET NOW

Okay, so here you are at the start of the wedding plans, celebrating the bride and groom's great news in a wonderful way to remember. Is this when you say, "Just so you know, I'm not made of money, so we're going to have to take it easy on the expenditures. No Jimmy Choos for me, okay?"

No, not just yet.

It's beyond essential that you communicate your need for smart budget choices as early in the process as possible, but timing is everything. You don't want the bride to go from elated to deflated (and irate) if she thinks the only reason you invited her over to your place for a home-cooked, gourmet dinner was to set ground rules with *her* about her wedding plans. Some brides really freak out at this premature revelation . . . because that might have been what her mother-in-law just did, ruining an engagement celebration with a sourpuss "Don't get too excited, I'm not made of money" smack-down on her plans and dreams. No, you don't want to go there. Again, timing is everything.

So when *do* you bring up your request to keep expenses on the affordable side? The week *after* you celebrate her engagement news with her. You've got to get in there early, and a week later is often ideal. Because some brides—like me—start planning right away. I researched my bridesmaids' gowns before I even found *my* wedding gown, since I was trying to lock in on the color scheme for my wedding. I had six dresses saved to my Favorites file before my engagement ring felt normal on my hand. Early contact is best.

With timing covered, now it's time for how to say it . . . which is all-important. In the center of most conflicts is this complaint from one warring party: "It's not what she said, it's *how she said it.*" Some battles begin because of wrong phrasing that one person blew up into an insult.

Now hear this: *You can't control how someone takes things.* All you can do is lessen the odds that what you mean to convey comes with a tacked-on message that hits the bride in one of her deeply hidden raw nerves. For instance, she might have a deep inner wound that no one listens to her. She's a pleaser. She's always been the Go-To girl in her family, and her bossy older sister always overruled her. So throughout her life, she's always been wary of those who might tweak her plans, turning everyone into a version of that bossy older sister. Therapists and family counselors stand behind me on this one, with the reminder that *you can't control how someone takes things.* So that's why you have to be very careful here. Get it right, and you're in great shape for a season of the bride welcoming your brilliant budget ideas that still look elegant and upscale. Get it wrong, and you're the bad guy.

That's a lot of pressure, but you can do it. Here are some ways to bring up the budget issue:

In *a phone call or in person*, not in an email or text, you'll start by congratulating her again and telling her how excited you are:

YOU: "I have to say it again, I am SO happy that you and Mike are getting married. He's such a terrific guy, and your wedding is going to be such a fabulous day."

HER: "It's going to be perfect! We're looking at places right now . . . our wedding coordinator is taking us to a few different sites this weekend."

YOU: "Anything I can do to help?"

HER: "If you know of any great ballrooms that have an outdoor terrace for the cocktail party . . ."

YOU: "I do! I'll email you the links to a few amazing places I've been to. They're gorgeous, and they're not too expensive."

HER: "Ooo, that's great. We're trying to take it easy on our parents . . ." (laughs)

Okay, you see where we're going here. The door is open. The money issue is out there. And *you* opened the door by saying the places aren't too expensive.

YOU: "Yeah, money's a challenge for most people right now, so I hope you'll be open to my suggesting some ideas on how we as bridesmaids can do an amazing job for you without spending too much. I have this book with lots of recommended websites and resources to cut prices in half, and I wanted to make sure I had your okay before I suggested anything to the maid of honor or to you."

If she's quiet right now, it doesn't mean she's deleting your number from her cell phone, de-friending you from her Facebook, and drafting a "You're fired" email to you. Most people would just listen right now, taking it all in. Especially if they're sensitive to other people's input about the wedding.

YOU: "You deserve everything to be top-shelf and fabulous, and I will do anything possible to help make everything perfect. I just know that my budget's always a little tight, and if I have access to insider secrets and phenomenal resources to save everyone a lot of money, I'd like to share them with you. Is that okay?"

HER: "Yes, of course! I'm sure all of the bridesmaids will *love* checking out the sites you have in mind. I don't want anyone to be upset about the money."

She's registered that you're honoring her by *asking*, which is something many people don't get enough of. Honor and respect.

If she's been in a bridal party before, she knows how bridesmaids want affordable options, so *you don't have to spell it out to her in any way that can be taken as talking down to her* . . . like this: "Well, Shelly's still in school, and Margaret's still paying off her wedding, and your sister doesn't have a job right now, so I'm thinking we need to be considerate of them." *Whoa!* The bride knows these things about her friends and her sister, and you don't have to educate her. She could be hearing some assumptions in there, namely *I don't think you'd be considerate of the bridesmaids*. And off she goes, fired up that you'd insult her in that way. Which you didn't. But that's what she absorbed. Gotta be careful, because this is one of the biggest mistakes bridesmaids make when trying to bring up the money issue.

You didn't insult her. You kept it very straightforward and to the point, simply asking if you can contribute your amazing collection of smart budgeting ideas and resources. And she said yes.

Now if she's vague, it's only because she's feeling out what you just said. *Wait, have I lost control of the bridesmaid plans already?* So you seal the deal with reassurance before her mind runs away with an imagined worry.

YOU: "Excellent! You're the bride, and I'm never going to step on your toes."

Ta da!!

YOU: "I didn't think you'd have a problem with it, but it's always best to ask first. Now tell me more about the places you're looking at . . ."

Brides say they hate it when their bridesmaids ask for reassurance that they won't have to spend a fortune, and once they get it, they're right off the phone.

Always, always follow up with excited conversation about the start of her wedding plans, what her groom wants, and all the fun details she's blissful over right now. If she deflated a little bit by your mentioning the reality of money, she'll puff right back up as she enjoys sharing her wedding plans with you. And of course, there's always talking about other things, like plans for Girl's Night Out next week.

With permission granted for you to share your best bridesmaid budget finds, you can relax and look forward to priority #1: the bride's enjoyment of this whole process. Money may seem like the center of it all, but it's mostly about your relationship. That's going to factor into a lot of your future work as a bridesmaid, which you'll read more about in future chapters. You just did a great job as a sister or as a friend, as a dream bridesmaid, by starting off asking the bride's permission for you to encourage great budget decisions. She's going to remember that for a long, long time. You *asked*. That's wonderful.

CHAPTER 2

Engagement Parties and Gifts

ithin weeks of the happy couple's engagement, you might find yourself invited to an engagement party. Or two. Granted, many wedding couples now choose to skip the engagement party—not wanting it to be seen as a plea for gifts from friends, or obligating their family members to travel . . . with a gift. They prefer to just go to dinner with their parents and their siblings instead, keeping it small and intimate and inexpensive for their parents to host. Some couples use this engagement dinner as their chance to have their families meet for the first time, or share in their excitement together if the families are already close. No need for a big party. The smaller get-together does just fine.

If this is the case, you've just saved the average expense of $100 or so, for travel, a gift, and maybe a new party outfit.

If this is not the case, if there is a party to attend, it's time to start putting smart budget strategies into use.

If there is a party to co-host and you live too far away to attend, you *do not have to split the cost of this party with other, local bridesmaids who are hosting.* Countless bridesmaids write to me with this dilemma, panicked as they are about such an early, pricey request. We no longer live in a society where we all reside in the same hometown, or just minutes away from one another, and while etiquette of yesteryear says that bridal party members are *required* to host and attend all pre-wedding parties, that's just not the case anymore. You're off the hook.

So if that well-meaning maid of honor emails you with an outline of plans and costs for the engagement party, you're well within your rights to respond with a polite, "Sorry, I won't be able to participate nor host this party, since I live in (state)"—which the maid of honor might not have even known from the list of names and email addresses given to her by the bride. Keep in mind: At this early stage, you'll be asked to be included in everything, as part of the maid of honor wanting to be proper and polite, and it's a mistake to assume that anyone's out to get you or your wallet. So if you've experienced grabby maids of honor before, give this one the benefit of the doubt.

If You're a Party Host

The maid of honor might call you up to explain that since the bride and groom currently live far away from their families, the task of planning an engagement celebration falls to her, and the bridal party is asked to help host it. Or *you* might be in the lead on this, as the bridal party member living in the bride and groom's hometown, and you know they'd dearly love an engagement party to share with all of their local friends. If hosting duties do fall to you, use the ideas in Part Two of this book, your collection of smart budget ideas for bridal showers, to plan the perfect get-together without spending a fortune.

Now, it's up to you if you want to send a small contribution to the party funds—which the maid of honor will so greatly appreciate—but you're not obligated to do so. Bridesmaids listen to their own inner voice of code of proper behavior on this one. Even though you're not required to help out with a small donation, you might not feel right not sending something.

Plus, when you're the far-away one and think it's okay not to do anything for that hometown party, you start to worry about not just the bridal party but also the bride's mother disliking your decision to save what probably would be $30 or so.

For your ultimate peace and decision-making status, again, it's actually quite smart to send a *little* something in your absence. Which doesn't come close to what it would cost for you to travel to the party.

Real Stories

Says one grateful maid of honor, "I knew the bride's friend lived clear across the country, working her butt off in medical school, and money was tight for her, so when she sent me a check for $25 to help out with the party plans, I made sure to call and thank her, and I decided to have that money go toward the cute cake we planned to order in the shape of a blue Tiffany box, the bride's favorite. She was beyond thrilled. We took pictures of the cake and texted them right to her during the party. I know if *I* was far away, working *my* butt off instead of being at a great party with friends and the bride and having fun, it would really make my day to get a text like that and be such an important part of the festivities even from so far away." If other bridesmaids can only contribute from their own distances in a modest way, make them feel included and an important part of the team, as well.

HELPING OUT THE HOSTS

Before we get into helping you choose a fantastic engagement gift on a budget—which is probably weighing on your mind right now, since you want to give something wonderful—let's cover the smart, *free* moves you can make to help the parents or other hosts with the party plans. Not all assistance has a price tag, but some can be quite valuable to the hosts.

Offer to help set up for the party, including the option of coming over the day before to clean the house (a great idea if parents are elderly or health-challenged). You might offer to help with any of the following:

- Making invitations on your home computer

- Providing them with mailing addresses for the couples' friends

- Sharing your favorite party supply sources and rental agency contact information

- Bringing over your platters and serve ware so the hosts don't have to rent supplies

- Cooking or baking a dish for the party

- Bringing pitchers for the making of sangria or iced tea

- Going to the liquor store to pick up and deliver cases of wine they've ordered

- Going to the store to pick up and deliver bags of ice

- Preparing outdoor party space, including hosing down deck chairs and tables, weeding flower beds, and helping with other yard and terrace improvements

- Working during the party to serve appetizers to guests, or to tend the bar, or to bring out hot catering trays to the table, or to set up the coffee and dessert bar

- Working cleanup duty

A Happy Fringe Benefit

One of the biggest benefits to devoting your time to the hosts of the party is that they get to know you better and may love your resourcefulness, which comes into play later when the hosts look to plan the bachelorette party, after-party, or wedding weekend events that you might be called in to help plan beautifully on a budget. You have to be in, or at least near, the planning circle to have any say in these types of extras. Volunteering to help at the engagement party could be your red carpet entrance to the circle.

"CAN I BRING A LITTLE SOMETHING?"

One of the best, most appreciated ways to contribute to the party is offering to bring a little something for the menu or bar. Here are the top five most crowd-pleasing and affordable covered dishes to bring, along with wallet-saving tips to cut the cost in half without the savings showing:

1. Fruit platter. Since so much of party fare is fried and fattening, the fruit platter is always a top draw. Cut your costs down, way down, by skipping the pre-arranged fruit platters in the refrigerator case at the supermarket—some of which can cost upwards of $30!—and create your own from scratch. A whole watermelon; two whole cantaloupes; a pack each of strawberries, raspberries, and blueberries; and fresh oranges. Your total is under $15, and you get that wonderful domestic bliss of slicing and cubing your own fruit.

2. Cheese platter. Again, buy bricks of cheddar, Colby, and other varieties and cube your own, spending one-third less than the prices of those pre-cubed packages (and getting far fresher-looking cubes!)

3. Dips. The crowd will love your spinach dip or hummus.

4. Brownie platter. Skip those premade, professionally iced brownies from your supermarket bakery and make two $4 boxes of the homemade stuff.

5. Two bottles of wine. Check WineSpectator.com for their lists of top wines under $15 a bottle, which turns out far better than you would expect!

There's a world of amazing, low-priced vintages out there, and you can trust this site's reviewers to steer you to phenomenal, crowd-pleasing wines on a budget.

GIVING A GREAT ENGAGEMENT GIFT

If your bridesmaid group is a collection of sisters and friends you already know well, it's well worth a call to the maid of honor (respecting her position as the recognized group leader) to suggest setting up a terrific group gift from the couple's registry. Have a few items already in mind, to be able to say, "We could get their cappuccino machine with all eight of us chipping in $30 apiece, so they can 'fuel up' for the fun planning months ahead." You know the bride loves her cappuccino, so what better early-stage gift than something she can really use? And, since that's a big-ticket item that most other guests are unlikely to select for the couple, you may have just prevented them from having to use their gift cards later to buy the same item. And you get the Wow Factor of being part of the group that gave the awesome gift. Many brides say their cappuccino maker was their number-one most-wanted wedding gift.

Not liking the idea of a group gift shared with the other bridesmaids? Resist the urge to spend too much on something fabulous from the registry. We all know brides who sign on for the $200 gravy boat. Don't be one of those bridesmaids who try to compete with the other bridesmaids. Just give the bride and groom a gift they'll be able to use during the wedding planning months, in good times and in bad (more stressful) times.

Here are some fabulous engagement gifts costing $25 and under:

• A pretty journal, in which they'll record their wedding-planning memories

• A basket of massage oils and lotions, in their favorite de-stressing aromatherapy scent. Throw in a gift card for a local Massage Envy (www .massageenvy.com) center for a free hot stone massage session, and your gift can be a rescue when wedding stress builds.

• A gift card to a restaurant—upscale or family-style like Applebees—for both de-stressing and celebration, since they might want to go out for a sangria to celebrate signing for their reception site

• A gift card to their local movie theater . . . perfect for a date night to keep the couple close as the wedding plans press onward

• A box of dark chocolate truffles for pure indulgence and a happy hormone rush

• A fine bottle of wine or champagne with a note to share this on the anniversary of their engagement, or to toast any other special occasion they have in mind

• A gift card to their favorite gardening center. Getting in the dirt is therapeutic, very relaxing. And if your bride loves potted herbs or her veggie garden, your gift gives her a fresh new session doing her favorite, relaxing thing . . . and maybe starts a garden in their new home!

• Anything off the registry with an entertaining component, like her chip and dip bowls or a great glass pitcher

• Another favorite off the registry: a fabulous throw blanket, such as a soft fleece throw that she and her groom can snuggle under while decompressing in front of a good movie. Throw in the gift card for that movie rental, too.

• Gift cards to their favorite healthy foods store. Brides and grooms *love* this one, so that they can afford those healthier organic fruits and veggies while they're spending so much of their money on the wedding.

Wait, a Gift Card?

Gift-givers on a budget often shy away from gift cards. After all, it's not too impressive when a big, red $20 is stamped on the card. That's the equivalent of leaving the price tag on a gift. But when you pair the gift card with assorted little theme items, like their inexpensive whisks and spatulas from the registry to go with that health food gift card, it magnifies the look and feel of the gift. That $20 chip and dip set takes on the essence of greater value when you add in pretty printed recipes for gourmet dips, which you can find and print for *free* at FoodTV .com. The gift card for the health food? Add in a subscription to a healthy cooking magazine, which you can often get for $10 or less. Magazine subscriptions are *great* engagement gifts, since they'll keep arriving every month and add to the couple's future married lifestyle. Plus, prices are fabulous now, and you can often find freebie gift subscriptions when you renew your own. No one has to know it was free.

"My bridesmaid knew I was planning to do a lot of DIY projects to save on our wedding, and when she gave me a gift card to the craft store, she also gave me the gift of *free* Save the Date cards! I couldn't be happier," says one bride. "That was a great idea. Not just the dollar value of the craft materials. That gift card allowed us to take a piece of our DIY budget and move it to the *cake*!"

"We received a lot of our china and crystal at the engagement party, which was wonderful," says another bride. "But one of my favorite gifts came from my bridesmaid Tara. She knows that I get stressed out very easily, and the thing that works the best to calm me down is a bubble bath. She gave us a basket of amazing, aromatherapy bubble bath bottles and included a note that this was to tame my wedding stress ... which, in keeping me sane, was also a gift to my groom! I can't even begin to tell you how much those bubble baths helped me relax and enjoy the whole wedding process." Tara spent just $15 at CVS for four pretty bubble bath bottles.

Now that's way better than a $200 gravy boat!

Gift Card Rewards

Check out your credit card rewards program. Many offer the chance to cash in some of your rewards points to get gift cards at discount. A $50 gift card to a restaurant might only cost you $25 with a certain amount of points cashed in. Or your card's points total might allow you to get that gift card entirely for free. Just read the fine print and allow enough time for delivery. Some cards send within a week, and others take months.

CHAPTER 3

Travel and Lodging Arrangements

*I*f you live in the same hometown as the bride, and that's where the wedding will take place, you're among the lucky bridesmaids out there who don't have to worry about travel expenses. These days, though, a great number of bridesmaids *do* have to make room in their budgets for travel and lodging.

According to a recent survey by TheWeddingReport.com, here's how far bridesmaids travel for the wedding, the bridal shower, and the bachelorette party—all of which take a chunk out of those budgets!

	WEDDING	SHOWER	BACHELORETTE PARTY
WITHIN 25 MILES OF HOME	35.51%	38.76%	32.61%
WITHIN 50 MILES OF HOME	16.40%	28.71%	24.35%
WITHIN THE STATE THAT YOU LIVE, BUT MORE THAN 50 MILES FROM HOME	15.51%	23.44%	20%
IN A DIFFERENT STATE	28.09%	6.22%	18.26%
OUTSIDE THE U.S.	4.49%	2.87%	4.78%

That's a lot of travel! You'll soon find out how you can save lots of money while getting to each event.

Even at a local wedding, many bridesmaids decide to get a hotel room for the night of the wedding, both for safety's sake—no driving after drinking at the reception—and also to share in the after-party action, socializing with the rest of the guests. No one wants to leave the party, so one night's hotel stay becomes a Must.

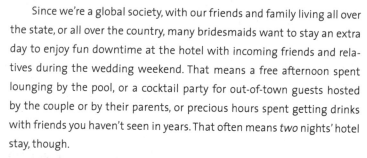

"Sorry, We Can't Pay for You"

In the past, wedding couples traditionally paid for the bridal party members' travel and lodging, but today that is not often the case. According to a survey at iVillage Weddings, 85 percent of wedding couples say they're *not* going to pay for all of their bridal party members' travel and lodging. Eleven percent said they'd pay for one or two bridesmaids or groomsmen who were having financial hardship, but not the entire group. Even some brides and grooms planning destination weddings say, "Make your travel expenses your wedding gift to us." While you might be among the lucky bridal party members whose travel expenses are covered by the bride and groom, don't count on it. Only 4 percent of wedding couples pick up that particular tab.

Since we're a global society, with our friends and family living all over the state, or all over the country, many bridesmaids want to stay an extra day to enjoy fun downtime at the hotel with incoming friends and relatives during the wedding weekend. That means a free afternoon spent lounging by the pool, or a cocktail party for out-of-town guests hosted by the couple or by their parents, or precious hours spent getting drinks with friends you haven't seen in years. That often means *two* nights' hotel stay, though.

And of course, there's the trend of destination weddings. The bride and groom may be among those who wish to invite a small handful of guests to an exotic location, or to a city or resort town just a few hours away, to cut down their expenses and have the getaway wedding of their dreams. That could mean increased expenses for you, such as plane fare, three or four nights' hotel stay, and more.

What Were Those Averages Again?

According to TheWeddingReport.com, the national averages for travel and lodging at the time of this writing were:

- $140 per night for the hotel stay
- $303 for plane fare
- $88 per night for a rental car

And again, that's just the national average. Depending on when a destination wedding takes place, or if the wedding you have to fly to occurs during the holidays or a peak travel time, you can easily triple that plane fare and double the hotel room price. Timing is something you have no control over, but you *can* take smart steps to cut down these expenses.

BEFORE THE WEDDING WEEKEND

If you live far away from the bride and her other bridesmaids, you may receive an invitation to go on that dream-come-true girls' shopping outing where the bride oversees the trying-on of potential bridesmaids' gowns. The bride has planned a champagne brunch and you're all supposed to go boutique-hopping to find the ideal gowns. *She wants me to fly in to go dress shopping with the group? Is she kidding?*

Saying no to this invitation if it would squeeze your available funds too tightly is an anxiety-ridden dilemma. You don't want to let the bride down, but it's just not realistic for you to spend over $300 to get to this particular activity. It's okay to say you can't make it. Most brides say they understand, that they would never want to harm their bridesmaids financially with a request like this one, and that technology—in the form of dress photos texted to the faraway bridesmaids—solves the problem. "The truth is, I knew she wouldn't be able to fly in, but I was doing the proper thing in inviting her," confesses one bride who felt for the faraway bridesmaid but still looked forward to the gown shopping trip with the rest of her bridesmaids.

You'll find gown selection budget-savers in Chapter 5, saving the day if you won't be able to fly in for the gown selection outing.

GET WITH THE GROUP

The bride and groom might not be aware of this, but they can arrange for group travel discounts as well as for discounted blocks of hotel rooms. American Airlines is one of the major airlines that offers group rates for weddings—often with additional group discounts on rental cars and other travel perks.

Ask the bride if she has heard about group airline discounts, and together you can research the possibilities of arranging discount fares for the group of ten or more people in your area who will be flying in for the wedding. True, it takes a lot of legwork to coordinate everyone's schedules, but these days, guests are all too happy to get an email from the bride informing them that she's working on getting discount airfare for guests in their area, and that one flight time needs to be agreed upon. If you're concerned that guests will find it impossible to agree on a time of departure, think about this: Corporations do this all the time when they're arranging group flights for their faraway conferences and retreats. So it can be done, and at the end of the day, you may earn 20 to 40 percent off your group's airfare, plus an extra 15 to 30 percent off car rentals.

Here's a fun one that saves a bundle: You may count as a destination wedding "group," without going to a traditional "destination wedding."

All it takes is one call to the airline, or help from a travel agent who can work some magic on your behalf, to get a destination wedding discount even if you're not flying to Jamaica or Bermuda, Hawaii or another island location. The travel industry knows that a quickly growing trend in destination weddings is staying on the mainland, traveling to a locale just a few hours away, in a major city or tourist area, or even in the bride or groom's small town hometown. When you or your agent explain that the destination wedding is in Chicago or Savannah or SmallandSweetville USA, *your group may be granted the same big discount as those headed to an exotic locale.* It never hurts—and it often pays—to ask, since airlines are very interested in attracting your group's ticket purchases and may be more willing to help you out.

Make It Easier to Group Plan!

Here's a great website recommended by *Travel & Leisure* that allows you to coordinate group travel: Triporama.com. When you sign on for *free*, you create a personalized webpage that lets you communicate with your fellow travelers, share comments on a personal message board, build an itinerary, and otherwise create your shared travel plan in an organized manner. The site also shows you current special discounts at an array of resorts and destinations, making this a smart tool to use in your group travel planning efforts.

Take It to the Rails

Don't count out the train! Amtrak offers group rates, too, so if the wedding is going to take place a few hours away, it's worth it to check out the rail line's specials and group rates. Many wedding groups find it surprising—since they may not travel on Amtrak as often as they fly—that the company offers some phenomenal special packages for weekend trips, such as fall foliage ventures to New England with rail fare blended with hotel discounts. Add in the party atmosphere of traveling with so many friends and family on the train, and the value added is exponential. You get extra mingling time with people you don't get to see all too often, and if you're a single bridesmaid, maybe those mingling hours will allow you chatting time with the hot groomsmen.

Are You in the Club?
Travel clubs like AAA also offer group rates, so if you're a member, and if others in your area are members, you could save a large portion of your travel expenses on plane or rail tickets.

SHARING TRAVEL EXPENSES WITH THE OTHER BRIDESMAIDS

Often, it's the maid of honor who suggests that the bridesmaids save money by driving into town together and sharing hotel rooms, but this is certainly a suggestion you can pose to her via email. Since she's in charge of the bridal party, it's always a good idea to respect her position and propose your plan to her first, asking if she'd like you to email the other bridesmaids to see who's interested. She may appreciate it, and she may decide to add your idea to an information e-blast she was already planning to send to the group.

For my wedding, two of my bridesmaids decided to carpool from Pennsylvania to my hometown in New Jersey for the wedding weekend, and they made it a fun and enjoyable trip for themselves and the husbands by stopping off at a winery along the way. They saved on a tank of gas—which cost a fortune at that time—and it meant the world to me that they were able to add a bonding social activity to the time they'd be spending on the road to my wedding weekend.

Now, how does saving 50 percent on your hotel bill sound? That's what you get when you and another bridesmaid share a standard hotel room with two double or queen-sized beds in it. Two couples can share one room as well. Another strategy is booking a suite that has two bedrooms and getting six people into the room. I wouldn't go much above six people, since it can be a real challenge for all of you to share the one bathroom (although some suites may have two bathrooms), and getting dressed for the rehearsal dinner could pose some space problems with all of the outlets taken up by various flatirons and phone chargers. Be wise in how many people you invite to share a room, and never attempt to rip off the hotel by putting four extra people on the floor. You don't want to get reported by housekeeping and booted out of the hotel. It has happened!

Four in the Room Brought Back Great Memories!

"Sharing the hotel room with three other girls brought back great memories of how we all shared a shore house for two weeks one summer, with four of us crammed into one bedroom. It was chaos, but for two nights it worked!" says one bridesmaid who saved over 75 percent on her share of the hotel bill.

. . . AND GET A FREE BREAKFAST, TOO!

Brides and grooms work very hard to create their hotel room discount blocks, collecting two or three different hotel blocks in different price ranges to suit their guests' personal budget levels. As the helpful bridesmaid, you might save the day by suggesting that one of those lodging sites be a bed-and-breakfast establishment.

Granted, not all bed-and-breakfasts are inexpensive—some feature rooms that cost twice the price of a hotel block room—but some offer terrific prices and special weekend packages that cost 20 to 40 percent less than the rooms in the ritzier hotels the bride and groom have chosen for their proximity. With breakfast being provided as part of the room rate, you may find in your research that a B&B gives the perfect price break and perks, and as the bridal party, you could take over a floor of the place, sipping mimosas on the terrace in the early morning or sitting by the fireplace together into the wee hours.

Ask about a group discount at the B&B, and it only gets better, with an extra 10 percent, 15 percent, or 20 percent off.

THAT'S WHAT THEY'RE THERE FOR!

The Board of Tourism at the wedding's location is a goldmine for savings... and freebies! It's not just big cities, islands, and foreign countries who have their own tourism departments where you can often find out about special discount rates; seasonal specials with steep price cuts; holiday weekend deals; low-price packages; and additional discounts granted to students, veterans, and other special groups. Some of these sites will send you packets of big-savings coupons and two-for-one deals for hotels, restaurants, and tourism spots to save you plenty on your additional expenses while in the area. The tourism board's website may have coupons for you to easily upload, saving you and others in the bridal party a nice amount of cash.

Go to TOWD.com to find the tourism board of any location you're headed to—city, town, country, or island—and here's another Insider Secret: Don't think that what's on the website is the entirety of the special offers and freebies you can find! Call the tourism office and explain that you're coming into town as part of a wedding group, and ask if they have special packets of discounts for bridal groups *and family reunions*. Taking this extra step can net you some fabulous freebies and even discounts on your hotel bill and car rental, extra perks that tourism offices are only too happy to offer.

If It's Free, It's for Me

"I didn't even know that we had a tourism office *here in our hometown where the wedding is!*" says one proud bridesmaid. "I called, explained that we were a wedding group looking for discounts at area restaurants and local businesses, and we got a bunch of $20-off coupons for the beauty salon where we'd be getting our hair and makeup done on the wedding day, as well as a half-off coupon for a great jazz club where we decided to bring the bride for a night-before bachelorette party of sorts. Since some of the other bridesmaids live far away, we never did a bachelorette party, so this great deal became our make-up for that, and the price was terrific!"

LET THE HOTEL HELP YOU SAVE

Check the website for the hotel where you wish to stay. Their special package rates might be priced at an amount that beats the wedding room block price! I've seen Romance Weekend Packages for $99 at a hotel that offered a $129 wedding room block rate, and you'd get a bottle of champagne and a box of chocolates in your room for free as part of the package. There's no rule saying you have to lock into the wedding block rate like everyone else, which would be silly when there are deals like this to be found.

If you stay often at hotels like Marriott or the Hilton, you might be a member of their rewards plan, and that might earn you an additional discount. "I checked with my date to see if he was a member of the Marriott hotel club, and he was! So we had him book the hotel room, for a third less than the hotel block rate, and I paid him back," says one genius bridesmaid.

Other bridesmaids say they forgot they had a hotel club card in their wallet! "I've been in graduate school for so long that I forgot that I joined the Hilton Honors club years ago. I fished out my card from my wallet, and I was able to get a great discount and points for future vacations."

What's in Your Wallet?

Your student ID card, your military ID card, the membership cards for any associations to which you belong, and your work ID card are often the magic tickets to great discounts you didn't even know you could get. When you go to your company's server or HR department or to the sites for business associations to which you belong, the Member Benefits page often shows *a list of discounts that you're able to get from airlines, hotels, office supply stores like Staples, and copy shops like Kinko's.* These discounts can net you 20 percent or more off of your purchases and travel arrangements, so dig through your wallet, talk to HR, and check those websites to see where you can save a bundle. And be aware that some employers and associations add new member discounts from month to month, so check back often and sign up for email or text notifications when new partner benefits are added to the list. You could save 50 percent on office supplies like papers for making shower invitations, copying, and also get great discounts on UPS shipping of bridesmaid gowns.

Another way that the hotel can help you save is through their special event discounts, which may or may not be listed on their website. For instance, if the weekend of the wedding is the same weekend as the first football game of the season in a college town, you might score a big discount on your room and enjoy free cocktail parties planned for guests.

It's Not Just College Football Games

Hotels might offer special discounts for the weekend of a big, annual festival—also to book up those rooms and sell lots of drinks at the bar—so check Festivals.com to see what might be going on in the wedding locale on the days you'll be there. That tourism board website comes in handy here again when you click on the Special Events and Community Calendar button!

FIND DEALS ONLINE

Booking your travel plans through discount sites online might not be anything new to you. It might be your usual way to book vacations and business trips, and you already have Expedia and Orbitz bookmarked. These sites are among the most popular and best-known out there, delivering phenomenal discounts for your airfare and hotel needs. Here are some of the big names in discount travel websites to check if you're not too familiar with the world of booking your own lower-priced fares and hotel stays:

- AAA.com (requires membership at a fee)

- Expedia.com (their Fare Alert tool tracks down flights for your chosen destination and your budget)

- Farecast.com (This site scans the historic pricing data for your airline, destination, and departure date, and lets you know if a fare is likely to go up or down within the week. You can spend $10 on FareGuard, which refunds the difference in price if the site tells you a price will dip and it increases instead; this site only includes forty-eight mainland cities, so check to see if yours is included before you sign on.)

- Farecompare.com (You enter what you want to spend and when you want to travel, and the site searches over 500 airlines to find you the best price.)

- Hotels.com

- Hotwire.com

- Kayak.com (shares discount deals on airfare, hotel rooms, and car rentals, and also allows you to browse an array of amenity details on the hotels you're currently researching)

- Orbitz.com (This site will monitor ticket prices for the flight you've booked, and if any other customer books the same flight at a lower price, Orbitz will send you a cash refund to make up the difference. That's a sweet deal, a nice surprise in the mailbox.)

- Sidestep.com (Owned by the same company as Kayak.com, this site delivers the best discount prices for your chosen departure time and destination.)

- Travelocity.com

- TravelZoo.com

- Vayama.com (A discount price site for international airlines)

- WeGoLo.com (When you search on this site, you'll get both the base cost of the flight and the fare, which includes taxes and extra fees such as per-bag costs, for over seventy-five low-price airline carriers.)

- Yapta.com (When you book your flight with the airline, this site will automatically monitor the fare, alert you if the price dips, and give you directions on how to acquire a refund for the difference from the airline itself.)

CAN I CRASH AT YOUR PLACE?

The one question that makes brides cringe when it comes to lodging is, "Can I stay with you?" Brides do feel guilty about how much money you're spending to be a member of the bridal party, and as much as they'd love to invite you to stay with them for free, it's quite an added pressure on them. "If I were to have a bridesmaid stay with me the night before the wedding, I'd be constantly concerned with being a good host, making sure they have their favorite drinks in the house, making sure there's always toilet paper in the bathroom, clean towels by the shower, and so on," says one bride. "No, I need to focus only on what I have to do for the wedding, and I can't worry about the place being messy. I've seen brides' rooms when they're getting ready—there's makeup containers everywhere, new stocking wrappers on the dresser. And if someone is here, I won't have any quiet time by myself, which I know I'm going to need." Staying with another friend or relative could be your fabulous free option and give you time to catch up with her, see her house, meet her kids, and enjoy time together. Just keep in mind: A good houseguest always brings a gift for the hosts. Always. A $10 box of chocolates, a bottle of wine, just a thoughtful gift.

DON'T STAY TOO LONG

At many weddings, the entire wedding weekend—a stretch of four days—is filled with planned activities such as a welcome cocktail party, a barbecue and His Side versus Her Side softball tournament, the rehearsal and rehearsal dinner, the wedding day events, and the morning-after breakfast. Some families add on a fifth day, inviting guests for an excursion into the city or to shopping outlets, on a guided tour of their town, or on a ski run or other activity. As a bridesmaid, you may feel pressure to attend every event, and that's fine if you can afford four nights in the hotel.

Most bridesmaids stay the night before and the night of the wedding. You're perfectly within your rights to let the bride know that your schedule allows you to arrive at noon the day before the wedding, and you'll have to leave right after breakfast on the morning after the wedding. You apologize, but you won't be able to join everyone for that very fun-sounding shopping trip in the city and sunset ski run.

You're not going to miss the big moments. It's okay to shave a nonessential day off of your stay, and save a few hundred dollars.

Speak Up Early

Let the bride know about your limited stay time as far in advance as possible. It would be a cruelty to spring your short stay on her a week before the wedding, when she's already ordered the food for that barbecue and bought you a team T-shirt for the softball tournament. Stressed-out brides don't like getting blindsided with plan shifts or letdowns right before the wedding.

WHEELS FOR THE WEEKEND

And finally, we get to the car issue. If you're not able to drive your car to the wedding location and use it while you're in town, or if you're a city-dweller with no need to own a car, you might face the need to rent a car for the wedding weekend. As you saw in the Introduction, bridesmaids' car rental averages $88. Per day. Not to mention any added fees, such as filling the gas tank before you return the car, plus an insurance plan.

The best solution is to coordinate a car-share plan with the other bridesmaids. You'll split the cost of the car rental and share it during the weekend, bringing your cost down to $20 or so. Using your club or work perks, rental fees might shave down an additional 20 percent or more, and when you choose to rent a non-flashy compact car you save even more. Resist the ego urge to rent the BMW. You don't need to turn heads with the car you're driving . . . you'll do that on the wedding day in your fabulous dress.

It Only Helps to Ask

The bride has so much on her mind, she probably hasn't even thought about how you and the bridesmaids will get to her house on the morning of the wedding, so pick a good moment weeks before the wedding to ask if she has any nearby friends who could volunteer to transport the bridesmaids to her place. Sometimes, the bride's father volunteers for this task, wanting to be of service in any way possible. Grooms have even stepped in to arrange for bridesmaid transportation. Don't pile into a cab with all of your dresses and shoes and makeup gear. Someone with a minivan is sure to save the day.

Before you start researching car rental rates, first ask if the hotel offers free shuttle service to and from the airport—many do, making your most crucial rides free. And ask the bride if she has arranged for the hotel shuttle bus to transport guests to and from the ceremony and reception sites. Sometimes, when the couple has a lot of out-of-town guests, the bride and groom arrange for such considerate and complimentary shuttle service, saving you a lot of money.

On the morning of the wedding, a friendly volunteer can bring you and the other hotel-staying bridesmaids to the bride's home—if she's not staying at the hotel, as well—for your beauty session, dressing time, and pre-wedding photographs. You might then all pile into the limousine for the ride to the ceremony.

Be warned that cab fare may be far more expensive at that location than what you're used to in your hometown, or even what you've experienced in other faraway cities. Some bridesmaids have shrugged off their transportation concerns with, "I'll just take a cab from the train station/airport/bride's house," and then they're floored when that simple ride from the train station to the hotel costs $60. Cabbies tell me that you can't always trust the "flat fare" quoted by a hotel that will call a cab for you—many are off by as much as $25. And then you're stuck. So cabbing it might not be the ideal plan for your budget.

Ask, too, if the hotel offers free parking for guests. The bride may be able to arrange for complimentary parking passes, or that tourism bureau can also hook you up with a freebie.

LITTLE EXTRAS

As you know from every vacation you've ever been on, a mountain of little extras pile up, sucking some of your trip budget down the drain. So here are some smart tips to save $20 here, $100 there:

• Make sure you know your airline's most current per-bag charges. Some airlines charge a lot per checked bag, and now the new scheme is to charge for carry-ons, so pack lightly with this in mind.

• Make sure you know what it costs to leave your car at the airport while you're away. Daily rates have skyrocketed, so you might be better off taking a $20 cab ride to the airport, or even having a friend drop you off . . . a favor you will return when he or she has a trip to take.

• Get your passport early, like now. It can take weeks to process a passport application for a destination wedding, and rush fees can reach up to $100 in some instances. It's an essential, so go check your passport's expiration date right now . . . you'd be shocked at how many bridesmaids know they have a passport but they think they have two more years until it expires. *Wrong!* Make sure you're all set way in advance, and save that wasted $100.

• Pack wisely. You know that if you need ibuprofen or maxi pads from the hotel gift shop, it's going to cost you an insane amount of money. Maybe there's a Target nearby, but maybe it's an hour away and you just can't swing out there. Bridesmaids say those little forgotten essentials have added up to an astounding $40 visit to the gift shop. And if you're driving to the destination, bring your own supply of bottled water, sodas, and snacks to save an additional $30 in on-site purchasing. "We brought a few bottles of wine with us, and we were able to host a little get-together for friends in our hotel room," says a resourceful and forward-thinking bridesmaid. "Had we ordered wine from room service, it would have cost over $120."

CHAPTER 4

Communicating with Other Bridesmaids

The rapport you build with the other bridesmaids can go a long way in helping you—and them—save money. You all have the same primary goal: to make the bride happy. And you all share a secondary goal: to do it without going broke.

Your Insider Secret here is that you can reach out to the other bridesmaids *right now* to suggest ideas for getting the best for less. Yes, the maid of honor is in charge, and it's not appropriate for you to overthrow her by sending out a "Here's how it's going to be" email to the group, appointing yourself as the Savings Guru. No one likes a bossy bridesmaid, after all.

But you're the one with this book in your hands, so *you can communicate to the bridesmaids that you have a collection of insider secrets and fantastic resources to help everyone get more for their money.* Before we get into the *how* and *when* of your most crucial message to the others, keep a few important things in mind:

1. **The bridesmaids all have different ideas of what's expensive and what's not.** You might all live in different regions of the country, or come from different financial backgrounds, so some of the bridesmaids might think $400 is a budget price for a dress. The others might gag a little bit thinking about spending that kind of money on a dress.

2. *The bridesmaids all have had different bridesmaid experiences*. For some, it might be their first time in the lineup, so they have no idea how things should proceed. For others, it's their tenth time in a bridal party, so they think *their* way is how to proceed. Some might have been thrilled with their prior bridesmaid experience, and some might have been scarred by skyrocketing expenses and a demanding bride.

3. *The bridesmaids all have different levels of assertiveness*. Some are quiet and agreeable, and some are aggressive and controlling, wanting things to go their way because they know best.

4. *The bridesmaids might be a wide range of ages*. You might have your nineteen-year-old college student, your twenty-something working women with a partying mind-set, and your thirty-something first-time moms with household budgets and kid expenses.

It's quite a group to partner with, quite a group to get on the same page. Especially if you aren't already close with everyone in the circle. Some bridesmaid groups have grown up together, and everyone knows that Danielle is "the bossy one" or that Bree is going to go along with whatever the group wants. That makes their group dynamic easier to predict. Everyone feels comfortable telling Danielle, "It's not your wedding, so ease up on the commands, okay?"

As mentioned earlier, the maid of honor is the leader of the group. You have to respect her, or she may fight every idea you have. "I waited a long time to be a maid of honor," says one bride's sister. "And I'm not going to sit back while this bossy bridesmaid over here tries to tell everyone that she knows what to do since she's been a maid of honor six times before."

My goal here is to help you *co-create* a smart communication plan that gets all of the bridesmaids working together as friends and partners, not splintering into warring factions that can't agree on anything or—sadly, it happens—competing over planning ideas to the point of *driving up* their expenses as everyone tries to outdo each other.

This horrific dynamic is best avoided by a smart communication plan between the bridesmaids. Here are the top tips for connecting and working with the group:

• After the maid of honor sends out an email to the bridesmaids, introducing herself and sharing her excitement for the bride and groom, *it's your time to Reply All with what you bring to the table.* That's right. Now's the time to write to all of the bridesmaids with, "Hi everyone! I'm (your name), and (bride) and I went to school together. I'm so happy for her, and I'm looking forward to meeting you all and working with you to make everything terrific for (bride). I have good news for you: I have a copy of the book *Bridesmaid on a Budget*, so I've already found a ton of great money-saving websites and secrets to help us all out when the shopping and party-planning starts! Looking forward to seeing you soon!"

• E-mail the maid of honor to offer your talents in DIY crafts or baking, letting her know about the money you can save the group. She can email the bridesmaids to ask about their talents as well. If you find out that Bree is known for her baking skills, her contribution to the bridal shower could save you over $150 in not having to order a cake.

• Ask how things are done in the bride's region. You might find out that potluck bridal showers are the norm in her area, which will save you a bundle. "I'm from the West Coast, and I thought potluck parties went out of style in the 1960s," admits one bridesmaid. "To me personally, asking someone to bring a dish to a party is super-rude, but when I got to the party and saw how happy everyone was to bring a casserole or an appetizer or dessert and how great it all turned out, it was quite a pleasant surprise." And she saved over $80.

• Agree to email, rather than call, with planning updates. Don't be afraid to tell the maid of honor that you'd prefer email updates rather than getting messages on your cell phone from her. Not only is email free—saving you on spent minutes with your cell phone plan—it provides you with an easily-researched record of who suggested what, when, and what that URL is.

• Speak up if the maid of honor seems like she plans to use Facebook or Twitter to communicate the dress shopping or shower plans with the bridesmaids. Sure, those might be easy modes of communication for her, as she creates a Group just for the bridesmaids, but it might not be your style to check in with Facebook ten times a day. Your Twitter feed might be so active that it would be easy to miss a Tweet from the maid of honor. So a simple, "I'd really like to do this on email, since Facebook sometimes drops messages, and I don't check in with it every day. I wouldn't want to miss an important message or a deadline from you."

• Make all ideas welcome. Maybe this should be number one, actually. All of the bridesmaids need to feel comfortable contributing their suggestions, so lead the way in thanking anyone who emails with an idea.

• Don't participate in insulting tacky ideas. Again, everyone has different bridesmaid experience and regional practices, so if you're against potluck dinners, word your response diplomatically: "I've heard that potluck parties are a lot of fun, but I know this isn't a style of party the bride's family would expect. So let's figure out some other ways to save on the shower catering. I have some ideas. . . ."

• See if you can invite all of the bridesmaids to share the planning on a webspace such as Microsoft Office Live's free tool that lets everyone log onto one dedicated site where you all post your suggestions and create your to-do lists. This way, everyone can follow along, see what's been done, answer questions, and easily find the information they need.

• Respect a no. What's low budget to you might not be low budget to another, so if a bridesmaid shoots down that dress that the others say they love, her no needs to count. You'll all keep looking.

• Handle conflicts between yourselves. Except for extreme cases of bridesmaid bitchiness or a growing *Mean Girls* dynamic in the group—at which point you might wish to speak to the maid of honor, or to the bride if the maid of honor is the one doing the *Mean Girls* thing—make a phone call to the troublemaker to ask her not to blow off planning lunches anymore.

Okay, so there's a number eleven: Talk with the bridesmaids about a Plan B for any decisions you make or ideas you plan to pursue. When you take the lead in suggesting a collection of Plan Bs, you save the day by preventing the kind of overspending that happens when a plan falls apart at the last minute. Things can go wrong with any party plans. If Costco doesn't have the sheet cake you planned to get for the shower, does the group approve of switching to your Plan B—the Costco cupcake platter with the pink frosting? When you're the one in the store a few hours before the party, you don't want to have to call every bridesmaid for the green light, nor do you want to head over to a bakery to get a sheet cake that costs three times as much. Pre-arranging the Plan B saves the day, and your budget.

Make Your List

Use the Plan B worksheet in the Appendix section of this book to get your bridesmaids communicating about a do-able plan in every area of your responsibilities.

CHAPTER 5

Getting Your Gorgeous Dress

*T*he dress is one of the first issues that arises for bridesmaids, and when the group starts searching for possible styles, you might look at the price before you even notice the dress's cut or color. According to TheWeddingReport.com, the average amount spent on a bridesmaid dress is $178, and your goal is to beat that number by far . . . and wear a dress that looks like you spent triple that amount. In this section, you'll find the best sources and secrets for getting moderately priced dresses that stand out as stylish and sophisticated, modern and marvelous.

BUDGET-FRIENDLY BASICS

We're taking your search step-by-step, to give you as much power as possible in the selection of your budget-friendly dress. If you've been a bridesmaid in the past, you might think that you have no say in the dress that's chosen for you, that the bride just sends you a link to the dress she wants you to wear. These days, that's pretty rare, since most brides want to give their girls a say in the matter. But inviting everyone to send gown choices, or descend upon a bridal gown shop en masse, can be quite scary to a bride who doesn't want total chaos and too many options for the bridesmaids to battle over. So, she might join forces with the maid of honor to search the Internet for lovely, affordable dresses, and then send you and the other bridesmaids five or six possibilities to choose from. Some brides only send three.

Can you steer them toward less expensive dresses than the bride's fashionista friends would vote for? Of course. You're always free to send the bride, early in the process, a few links to dresses in the collections you've discovered through this book. She might be grateful that you saved her hours of searching, and scouted out an amazing style at under $100. And she may look a little further into that source or collection and find additional well-priced dresses to show the others. You save her a ton of time, and you've done your job as a helpful bridesmaid well with your note "just sharing a few dress finds that everyone might want to consider."

Or, the bride might thank you for sharing, but go on and search for dresses her own way. It's a bridesmaid reality that you *might* get a say, but the ultimate decision always rests with the bride.

Matching or Custom-Choice?

The next big issue right at the start is whether or not the bride wants all of her bridesmaids in one matching style of dress, or if she's one of those brides who allows her bridesmaids to choose different bodice and skirt styles to suit their shapes ... and budget. This is a big trend right now, since brides do want their bridesmaids to be happy with their dress purchases, and maybe that bridesmaid with the 42DDD chest would rather wear a more flattering top than a strapless one.

Can you ask the bride if this will be a possibility? Yes, of course! But again, the bride might already have her mind made up. (As I mentioned earlier, I chose my bridesmaids' dresses, with the help of my maid of honor, weeks before I even started looking for my own dress!) You serve yourself and your budget well when you send that email or make that call, telling the bride you're excited to see what she has in mind for the dresses, and you were wondering if she's going to allow everyone to choose their own style of tops. She might not have thought about that idea, but perhaps she'll keep it in mind as she and the maid of honor search the styles online.

Always remember that a bride may have had an image of her all-matching bridesmaids in mind since she was a little girl, and she doesn't want anyone messing with her dream. So if you hear a no, honor her choice. It's a grave bridesmaid mistake to try to railroad the bride over this, so early in the process, becoming the first troublemaker to stress her out. Ask, but don't push, even if you think your way is best.

Fitting the Formality

The bridesmaids' dresses need to complement the bride's gown and suit the formality of the wedding. So the price of the dress will be affected by the formality of the big day. For an ultra-formal wedding, you'll be in long gowns that often cost more than cocktail dresses. For an informal outdoor wedding, you might be in a $35 sundress.

It's not an automatic rule, though, that a gown is always going to cost less than a dress. Depending on the designer, and where you get your dress, you may find a $100 gorgeous gown shown right next to a $300 cocktail dress. So don't fear that the bride's decision to have you in a long gown means you'll spend a lot more. Great bargains exist in every style of gown or dress, so we're going to treat them all as equals in this chapter.

But just as an FYI, it *is* appropriate at a formal wedding—afternoon or evening—for the bridesmaids to wear knee- or cocktail-length dresses if the bride is in a floor-length gown. They work for the formality, so you might get to wear a very re-wearable cocktail dress.

Now here's some more good news: a floor-length, tea-length, or even a hi-lo dress can be altered after the wedding into a re-wearable knee-length dress for just a small amount of money in alterations. So if you're prescribed a long gown, don't consider it a lost cause. Some bridesmaids have straps added, change the neckline, and even dye a pastel-colored dress black to make it the ultimate re-wearable.

No Clashing Colors

For a very long time, bridesmaid dresses were ordered in one place at one time, so that all the dresses would be made in the same dye lot and thus match perfectly. That's *still* a leading practice today, and the bride may have all of the bridesmaids send in their measurements to a bridal shop along with a deposit check or instructions on how to pay the shop directly.

Some brides will give out color swatch cards that they've ordered from their dress designers—like Dessy's fabulous color-match cards—to show bridesmaids which shade of blue is The One, by name and design number. And some will send a link to the exact shade of cranberry-colored dress to order from a website, with no worries about everyone being included in one order. Some brides prefer to give their bridesmaids ordering freedom, and not saddle their maid of honor with a complicated group order. Your essential budget information, then, is finding out from the bride how she plans to orchestrate the order, so that you know if you'll pay extra for shipping from the maid of honor's home and other price add-ons that arise from the bride's color-matching order wish.

A Dress You Can Really Wear Again

Once you know the formality and length, as well as the ordering plan the bride prefers, the next big consideration is *Will I be able to wear this again?*

If you're going to spend $150 on a bridesmaid dress, it becomes a $75 dress if you wear it to two events. And a $50 dress if you wear it to three. The ultimate goal when selecting a dress is to choose a style you're definitely going to want to wear again, thus making your investment very much worth it. Groups of bridesmaids actually vote on the suggested gowns being emailed to the group, with "multi-wear" as one of the deciding factors. A peach, polyester dress with full lace sleeves? Probably not going to get too many "multi-wear" votes. A strapless, black, A-line cocktail dress? That's going to get the votes, and your purchase means you now have something fabulous to wear to the office holiday party, or to a winter formal, or to your cousin's formal evening wedding next winter. So that $120 dress is well worth it. And if you can get it for $100 using a RetailMeNot .com coupon, that's even better.

Re-wearing, though, isn't every bridesmaid's goal. According to TheWeddingReport.com, there are a *lot* of bridesmaids out there only getting *one* wear out of their dresses: 81.3 percent of them, in fact. Here are the survey results for those who are getting *more* than one wear out of their dresses:

- 13.04 percent are wearing their dress or gown between two and five more times
- 5.43 percent are wearing their dress or gown between five and ten more times
- 22 percent are wearing their dress or gown more than ten times

Before you think that these bridesmaids are unwise with their dress choices—or stuck with ugly, poufy gowns chosen by fashion-challenged brides—keep in mind that many bridesmaids *donate* their gowns to fabulous charities like the Cinderella Project (providing gowns for low-income teens to wear to their proms) or Brides Against Breast Cancer (consignment-selling donated gowns to raise money for cancer research). So they're doing a good thing, and often getting a nice tax write-off for their donation. Others are selling their gently worn, stain-free gowns on eBay or at consignment shops to earn back a percentage of their dress investments. These options are up for your consideration, as well. There's no rule saying the only way to get more value from your dress is to wear it multiple times.

So *if* your group votes on and chooses a dress you're not likely to wear again—even as a costume—be comforted in knowing that you *can* get some of your money back, and maybe get a lot more than money in return when you donate yours to charity.

Which kinds of dresses meet your re-wearable status? The top choices in style for a dress you'll wear again are: knee-length or cocktail-length, with a strapless top or a straight-across bodice with thin straps. For a long gown, column-style is best. Simple and basic, in style every year. If you choose trendy designs such as ruching at the waist, ruffles, or bows, you're at the mercy of an ever-changing fashion tide. (Although, again, your alterations specialist can remove those accents and sleek your dress into a fashionable "new find.")

The top five colors that make a dress or gown re-wearable are: black, navy, cranberry, aqua or turquoise blue, and a deeper pink than a cotton candy pink. Fashion often brings us the resurgence of a new, hot color every year—it may be buttercup yellow or eggplant—and brown seems especially to come in and out of vogue very often. So if your group is torn between the deep pink dress and the popsicle orange, speak up and sell that deep pink re-wearable to the other bridesmaids mentioning exactly that: A great pink dress is going to give you multiple wears for two or three years, stretching your dress dollars and saving you several $100 dress purchases in the future.

Friendly Fabrics

Does the fabric of the dress matter much in pricing? Somewhat. You'll find plenty of dresses in fabulous cotton that cost a bit less than silks, and organzas and chiffons do cost more per-yard than dress cottons. Gown shop experts say that taffeta is trending up right now, since it's an inexpensive fabric that reflects color and looks gorgeous. But again, it's always going to be the designer and the detail, as well as where you buy the dress, that will determine how much it will cost. A dress with lots of layers, requiring more fabric, will cost more as well. So, be prepared to spend a bit more for a floor-length gown in a high-quality fabric with a few flowing layers. It's *good* to pay more for a dress made with quality materials; the dress hangs well, moves well, and has a pretty sheen that makes your bridesmaid group's dress choice stand out as high fashion, even if you landed a dress for under $100 from a great resource, using all of your *extra* resources.

So what are the great fabrics to look for? I spoke with several gown designers who say that bridesmaids are happiest in comfortable, soft, smooth, and flowing fabrics such as:

- Charmeuse
- Chiffon
- Cotton
- Crinkle Chiffon
- Eastern Shantung
- Shantung
- Taffeta

Again, taffeta makes the list as one of the better-priced fabrics, and cotton is on the list as well, as both an informal and a formal dress choice that keeps its shape and makes the green-weddings crowd happy. Speaking of eco-friendly gown fabrics, you'll find some designers showing gowns and dresses made from natural silk, natural cotton, and bamboo. Yes, these may be at a higher price point because they're not usually mass-produced overseas, but the extra expense is worth it when you know your dress is friendly to the earth, soft and luxurious, and ultimately re-wearable.

As important as it is to budget for quality fabrics, a bigger budget concern when it comes to fabrics is how difficult it is to *alter* a dress made from the more challenging fabrics. Seamstresses say they'll charge more for organza and chiffon, which can be very difficult and time-consuming to pin and sew during the alterations process. The same goes for intricately beaded sections of a dress such as a bodice or a beaded hem. In these cases, the seamstress may have to remove beads by hand, adjust the bodice, and then resew those tiny little beads back on to match the existing pattern. That's going to cost you!

A Shocking Alterations Secret

It costs a *lot* to raise the armholes on a dress! Petites often need higher armholes for their dresses, and it's a lot of work for the seamstress to make that adjustment look natural. So if you're petite, order a petite gown *that specifies petite dimensions in the arms, shoulders, and chest, not just the length*. This insider secret can save you hundreds! (Other surprisingly expensive alteration jobs: lowering an empire-waist seam to give you more room for your size B+ chest and fixing the back of a princess-seamed dress with vertical seams.)

BRIDESMAID ON A BUDGET

If the bridesmaids submit beaded chiffon or organza dress possibilities to the bride, speak up and tell everyone: You learned from this book that those fabrics can be *very* expensive in the alterations stage, sometimes three times as expensive as a less challenging fabric.

While we're on the subject of fabrics, it's *important to avoid cheap fabrics*. Yes, you could get a $30 designer dress from a discount store, but when that dress is made from a low-quality, itchy polyester that *looks* cheap from across the room, it's not a smart budget move. Remember, we're searching for the best *quality* dresses for an affordable price. So while it's exciting that Zac Posen and Jean Paul Gaultier are designing for Target, and some of these dresses are ultra-pretty, be aware that a pretty dress seen online might feel very uncomfortable to the touch.

Does this mean the designer collections at Target and Kohl's are out? Not at all. I searched through the pretty Zac's and Jean Paul's at Target and found some fabulous-quality cotton dresses for $39. Perfect as a bridesmaid dress find, and also ideal for a pretty, new rehearsal dinner dress. You *have* to look at fabrics to spend your money well.

Dressing Up a Simpler Dress

When your group selects a simpler style of dress, less expensive because it doesn't have detailed ruching or beading (that can raise the price by 25 percent!), you can make your dresses look twice as expensive by adding a pin-on brooch with sparkle. Many brides are giving their bridesmaids the sparkly pin to wear as a dress accent, and then keep as their thank-you gift. Other inexpensive additions that might be gifted to you, or added to your order, are matching or contrasting sashes, or faux floral pins that the bride selects for you.

Plus-Size and Maternity Dresses

Designers are now far friendlier to the fuller-figured and baby-bump bridesmaids out there, offering lovely dresses and gowns in many of the top collections, including big-name bridal lines and at department stores. I saw fabulous, fine fabric plus-sized dresses at Macy's for $99. With a bride who allows all of the bridesmaids to choose their own styles of dresses, these "specialty" dresses can be counted into a group order at a bridal shop, allowing you to be included in the savings and not cast away from the group to shop on your own. Discuss with the bride that you've heard this option exists, so that *she's* aware of it and adds it to her gown selection plan. Some brides simply don't know that their chosen gown source *has* maternity styles or plus-size dresses. Speaking up saves you money, and may just get the group shopping at a more affordable website where everyone's sizes can be fulfilled.

WHERE TO SHOP

And now we get into it . . . finding the best places to get your beautiful, budget-friendly dress. We'll take them one category at a time, since there are secrets to finding a steal at each of these types of locations. But first, I wanted to show you the results of my own recent search at some of the more popular sources for bridesmaid dresses.

Is there a time of year when bridesmaids' dresses are less expensive? You'll find great sales at prom time—March through May—and even bigger price cuts when the wave of prom-shoppers has moved through the racks, but left some gorgeous dresses behind. I've found pretty cocktail dresses perfect for bridesmaids at 75 percent off. Would it be smarter to wait until May to shop? Well, the post-prom bargains can also mean fewer dresses on the rack, making it harder for each of the bridesmaids to get her own size. So those prom-peak weeks could make this easier on you when there's a greater selection.

But that's just one time of year. An advantageous time to shop in stores and online, but a limited time.

Another time of year when bridesmaid-appropriate dresses are on sale is November through January, when winter formal dresses are priced attractively to move stock. You could find a fantastic jewel-blue dress for 60 percent off on the store's website, and email the maid of honor to let all the bridesmaids know about it. (Again, rack shopping at sale time might not have enough dresses in enough sizes to suit the entire group of bridesmaids, so the website could be your salvation.)

One Style of Dress, Huge Price Differences

Comparison-shopping for bridesmaid dresses is going to depend on where you look and *when*. I hopped around online, *at the height of prom dress season in April* when prices on party dresses were at peak, to comparison-shop for one type, length, and color of dress and found some huge differences that might just surprise you:

My target: a simple, blue, strapless cocktail dress, with no additional accents or beading

The results:

Macy's: Strapless "Soprano Dress" with a ruched front: $38.00, on sale for $27.99

Bloomingdales: ABS "Blake Dress": $240.00

Neiman Marcus: Herve Leger cocktail dress: $995.00. No joke.

David's Bridal: Straight, sleek cotton dress with back tie: $99.00

Kohl's: "Speechless" dress with pleats: $68, on sale for $47.60

Ann Taylor: Celebrations Bridal collection party dress, $215.00—in a few weeks, this dress will likely be on sale for $78, like it was last year!

HouseofBrides.com: Alfred Angelo dress: $156.00, on sale for $92.00

That Macy's one surprised you, didn't it? It floored me, and I went right out to buy one for this season's weddings I'm attending.

As you can see, the prices are all over the map, which proves one thing: Looking for your dress is going to take great timing, lots of searching, and checking out sites and stores you might not expect to offer budget-priced dresses and gowns.

Coming up in this chapter: Timing smarts still net you huge discounts, but you're not tied to the calendar. (You're going to love it!)

Bridal Shop Secrets

If you read a lot of bridal website articles and blogs, you've probably been warned away from bridal shops as the most expensive locations possible. But these shops have read those sites, too, and they're now putting together fabulous collections of moderately priced bridesmaid dresses, not to mention sale racks for dresses that are in their last months of availability. So don't count these elegant bridal shops out entirely. When you explore them with the bride, perhaps after you've sat on the couch to help the bride select her own gown, you may find a perfectly priced winner.

As an added perk, that bridal gown shop might grant a fantastic group rate for the bridesmaids' dresses when the bride buys her gown from them. So those $200 bridesmaid dresses might be available to you for $150, which could be in your budget ... and it gets even better when the shop offers free alterations on your dresses. More bridal shops are fighting off those "don't shop there" message board posts—and beating their competitors—by establishing great incentives for bridesmaid gown shopping with them.

There's another good reason to walk into the bridal shop: Get on their mailing list. When you sign up and provide your email address, you'll get early, VIP, members-only notification of trunk sales where you can find fabulous bridesmaid dresses for up to 75 percent off. Designers want to unload their this-season's collections, so they'll bring racks and racks of pretty gowns (plus shoes and accessories!) for you to browse. Keep in mind, though, that many designers' trunk sales offer just what they bring to the store. You might not be able to get seven dresses for all of the bridesmaids. But if you're in a smaller bridal party of just three or four bridesmaids, this could be your super-sale. And some designers *will* take your order for a 2, 8, 12, and 16 in the style of dress you find. They're showing, so they make the rules.

Bridal-Dress Web Sites

When you visit bridal websites, you'll find that many of the gowns shown do not have prices next to them. That's because a great number of designers don't wish to sell through websites, but instead want you to go to bridal shops to make your purchases. You're supposed to fall in love with a dress, then arrange for a group visit to a bridal shop, and *then* find out if the dress is in your budget. If not, you'll likely spend more to get it.

That might work for your group, or you can save time and money by going to special bridesmaid dress websites like Bridesmaids.com, where you'll find designer-line dresses *with the prices*. And at this site in particular, the discounts are *very* attractive. For example, I visited Bridesmaids.com and found the following:

- An After Six cocktail-length, strapless, chiffon dress with a drape surplus bodice for $129, down from $179

- An Alfred Sung cocktail halter dress in peau de soie, for $117, down from $154

- A Bill Levkoff black chiffon cocktail dress for $129, down from $170

- And so many more, I could go on and on.

I spoke with Elizabeth Andrei, owner of Bridesmaids.com, and found out that they're carrying Cynthia Rowley's new line of budget-priced bridesmaid dresses designed for the Dessy group. And Elizabeth says that Liz Fields is a hot name to look for as a fresh, new designer of affordable bridesmaid dresses. On this site, I found her matte satin cocktail length dress for $132, down from $184. And a Liz Fields empire-waist gown with a shirred bust, optional spaghetti straps, and a matching shawl included for $168.30, down from $198.

Yes, Cynthia Rowley is among the elite dress designers partnering with existing bridal fashion companies with her Dessy line. And a name you might know well—Vera Wang—is partnered with David's Bridal to make a line of affordable dresses available through their site and at their stores. Vera has caught on to the trend of bridesmaids shopping for their dresses online, and I'm sure a big wave of other designers will follow her lead.

A look at Watters and Watters bridesmaid dresses that the bridal magazines feature in bright candy colors, worn by beaming bridesmaids, might depress you when you see a bunch of $225 pricetags as the *starting* costs in that collection, but click on the Watters site's *Wtoo Bridesmaids* link for their budget-priced, fabulous dresses starting at $180. (Yes, that $180 is still a bit high, but you get dupioni silk and multi-wears from *these* dresses! And they look like $250 dresses!)

An important factor for ordering your dress is to go by *their* size chart, since the 10 you wear could qualify as a 14 in the designer's own formula of bust, waist, and hip measurements. Always search the site for their size chart, get your measurements taken professionally by a seamstress or at your local dry cleaner, and order your dress in the *right* size . . . so that you don't have to spend extra money exchanging it for a new one, and possibly paying $50 to $80 in rush fees!

Department Store Secrets

Earlier in this chapter, I mentioned the prom dresses at department stores. In addition to the prom gown racks, there's always the formal dress section, the party dress section, and the junior's party dress section that can fulfill your dress needs. Add on a store coupon, and shop during the weekend super-sales that department stores hold quite often, and you can get a fabulous dress for over 50 percent off.

Here's a fun secret about department stores: Many—like Macy's, Lord & Taylor, and Bloomingdales, among others—have personal shopper services, through which you're assigned a stylist who will interview you about the kind of dress you want and take your sizes, then collect up a dozen or so dresses for you to try on. When you say you're on a budget, he or she will pull phenomenal styles that are on discount, sometimes even the *dresses they haven't put out on the racks yet.* It's a free service. They work on commission. And they'll also gather up shoes and accessories for you, at budget prices, as well. Check the Resources section to find department store sources to check out, and you could get the celebrity treatment while you're saving hundreds of dollars.

Don't forget that department stores have their own bridal and bridesmaid collections! I spotted a gorgeous $89 red strapless satin cocktail dress at JCPenney.com, and the JC Penney store brand JonesWear showed a lovely charmeuse tie-waist dress in mango for $69.99, plus free shipping.

Department Store Sale and Coupon Alerts

You know that department store sales and coupons can get you designer buys for less, so check each site for their text alert programs, such as JC Penney's mobile coupon service, and don't miss a great offer!

Clothing Companies Going Bridal

Some of the top clothing companies such as J. Crew and Ann Taylor have leapt into the bridal market by establishing wedding collections that include affordable bridesmaids' dresses. J. Crew's Weddings & Parties Collection started off as a great option for destination weddings, but now their stylish dresses are at the top of brides' picks list because it's so easy for bridesmaids to order their dresses online and have them shipped directly to them. No time-consuming collection of size cards and deposit checks for one group order at the bridal shop.

You have to look carefully at these sites, since some of the newest designs will still be quite pricey at such sites as Ann Taylor, where a pretty Celebrations dress can retail at $200. But keep that page bookmarked, because those dresses go on sale often. For more than half off. The same goes for the dresses at J. Crew.

I looked at the J. Crew collection and found some absolute steals that beat that national average dress expense by far: a silk taffeta "Clementine" dress for $99.99, down from $215. A strapless silk taffeta "Lorelai" dress for $149.99, down from $215. A pretty coral-colored "Erica" dress for $79.99, down from $225.00. In silk tricotine, their "Sophia" dress was priced at $69.99, down from $165. Their "Allegra" dress was $159.99, down from $225.00.

I found the gems. On sale. Amidst the pricier $250.00 silk taffeta dresses and $425.00 silk chiffon floor-length gowns. A bride would flip out to find those, so you might want to send the J. Crew URL to your bride!

Oh, and shipping was *free*.

Here are some clothing stores that you might not have thought of as fabulous sources for your *bridesmaid's* dress—since you shop them for your other clothing needs—which makes them an incredible discovery for their budget-friendly styles:

• White House Black Market: Has a stylish line of bridesmaid dresses, and their shoe and purse collection is also white-hot in the savings department.

• Anthropologie: Their dresses collection shows lovely prints and ruffle knee-length dresses for $78 or so, perfect for destination and informal weddings . . . and also for your rehearsal dinner dress.

• The Limited: In addition to their pure silk and cotton dresses for the bride, you'll shop from their Fun and Flirty line (a current style shows a trendy ruffle-front dress cut just above the knee in bright poppy, gothic, or green lagoon), as well as their figure-flattering draped waist tank dresses in periwinkle or turquoise. Again, ideal for any type of wedding, and for your rehearsal dinner dress.

• Forever 21: That's right. They're not just tank tops and skinny jeans. This store has some fantastic bridesmaid dress finds.

Get Lucky!

If you subscribe to *Lucky* magazine, you know it's all about fab fashions, steals and deals, and the latest celebrity collections and trends. But here's where *Lucky* brings you great bridesmaid luck: Log on each day to see what their Deal of the Day is, and you—and the other bridesmaids—can score your dresses (or shoes) for 50 percent off.

Discount Stores

If I scared you about the polyester dresses at Target, Kohls, and Marshalls for $19 or $30, I meant only to get you to look at the fabric of the dress. It's still a smart idea to look at these fabulous budget fashion sections to scout out dresses like the *beautiful* Mossimo black crossover empire dress, almost entirely cotton, touchable and comfy, in eggplant for fall, for $39.00. There *are* gems at these stores, so be a Fabric Investigator to scout out the nice fabrics from the itchy polyesters, and you could save everyone hundreds on your dresses!

Outlet Stores

Outlet shopping can save you more than 60 percent on your bridesmaid dress, especially if your bride has given you the freedom to choose your own style of little black dress or strapless blue dress. You may have success shopping as a group, since outlet stores do stock large collections of gowns and dresses in different sizes, so this may be a winning destination for all of you.

To find a dress outlet store near you, or within a worth-it hour's drive, visit OutletBound.com.

Shipping

Shopping is expensive, and *shipping* is expensive. So keep the following tips in mind for anything you may have to send out, such as the other brides-maids' dresses that you pick up at the bridal shop:

• Go to UPS and ask for a frequent shipper card—or use the one you already have!—to get credits that will add up to free shipping for a future send.

• It's perfectly okay for you to email the maid of honor and ask her to remind the bridesmaids that they need to send you their checks for shipping their gowns to them. Include your mailing address on your send to her, so that she can just forward your message easily and quickly to all of the bridesmaids.

• Copy all receipts and keep them as a record of who needs to pay you back. A great plan is to scan the receipts and email them to the brides-maids for fast payback, with instructions on how to pay you. Keep in mind that some settings on PayPal take out a percentage for a processing fee, so checks may be best.

• Insurance is a smart purchase, especially for those bridesmaids' dresses or other important wedding items you're sending, so tell the bride ahead of time that you will get insurance and tracking numbers for each package you send, and when you give each bridesmaid her receipt, the low insurance fee will be on there, as well. Send the bride and each bridesmaid their own tracking numbers so that *they* can look up their packages' where-abouts on the UPS or Federal Express websites. Don't skip these essential investments, because if a dress gets lost in shipping, it's going to cost you many more times the cost of postage to replace it in a hurry!

What's the Rush?
And What's It Going to Cost You?

If your group waits too long to order your dresses from a bridal shop or website, it's going to cost you. Be aware that your version of late is different from designers'. At one top bridal site, I saw rush fees of $50 for a hurry-up delivery of *seven to eight weeks*. Super-rush, delivering the dress in five to six weeks, cost $80. Some bridesmaids get their *dresses* for that much! So shop early and save.

CHAPTER 6

Shoes and Accessories

*N*o one wants to spend $79, $99, $129 on those bridesmaid shoes from the dress salon, all dyed to the "perfect" shade of salmon or cobalt blue, knowing those heels will never see the light of day (nor the moonlight) again. So even though you're being led right now to some amazing sources for half-priced, *high-quality* shoes, the wear-again factor always has to sit at the forefront of the group's shoe decision.

You'll usually have a bride that takes the lead on the *Big Shoe Decision*. Will she decree that you'll all buy identical styles, color, and heel heights of one particular style in one particular designer's line? Or will she be That Bride who says, "Just go pick out whichever silver, strappy, open-toed heels that you love and that feel best to you, and everyone will wear their own style of shoe that they find at their own budget level." Brides like this are fabulous. Because some bridesmaids *already own* perfectly appropriate silver, strappy heels from the last time they were bridesmaids or from a wedding or formal they attended. Their investment now is a big, fat *$0* if they can wear their own shoes again. Check those shoeboxes up high in your closet. You might have the perfect pair of barely worn silver heels, saving you over $100.

SHOE SHOPPING SOURCES

Where do *you* buy your shoes? If you're like most women, you like to get your new shoes at a discount, and you have your favorite sources for doing just that. So we're going to go through those sources, and you'll find out how to maximize even bigger discount potentials.

Department Stores

You thought I was going to start with Payless? I'll get there. My first instinct is always to go after top-quality, designer shoes at huge discount prices, giving you the sturdy construction, the comfort, and the sizing you're used to in your favorite shoe brands, before you go to no-name brands that may line the discount shoe store sale racks for $6 apiece. We're going for Nina, Chinese Laundry, and other designers you love.

And When You Add the Coupon Code . . .

Just one visit to RetailMeNot.com or CouponCabin.com could net you an extra 20 percent off or more on your shoes purchased at department stores, or through a department store's website (since some coupon codes are for online-only purchases). If you do order shoes through a site without a try-on, make sure you'll be able to return them for a fall refund if they don't fit ideally. Read that small print, and don't throw away $40 on those super-sale shoes that squeeze your feet and can't be returned, the sad surprise that meets some bridesmaids who don't do their smart-shopping homework before clicking Buy.

Department stores like Nordstrom, Macy's, and Lord & Taylor have giant shoe sale events several times a year. When you get on their mailing lists—which you can sign onto at their websites—you'll get advance, VIP emails or postcards inviting you to their 60 to 75 percent-off members-only sales. Take that $120 pair of Chinese Laundry strappy heels, slash off 75 percent and that's $30. The same price as that no-name brand at the no-name shoe store in the strip mall. Considering that department store shoe sales often allow you to use the coupons you have, you might get an extra 10 percent or more off of that. Not bad.

And don't forget those department store personal shoppers whom you can work with *just to find your shoes!* The score? Often 25 to 40 percent off.

Outlet Stores

If I told you that you could get a $200 pair of designer shoes for $40, but all it would take is a half-hour drive to an outlet store you didn't know was there, would you go? Of course! Pile those bridesmaids into the car, and you *all* can go. Big savings for everyone!

Visit OutletBound.com to locate nearby outlet stores that open up a world of discount shoe finds at such store brands as:

- Aerosole
- Aldo
- Bakers
- Bare Feet
- Battaglia
- Brand Name
- Burlington Shoes
- DC Shoes
- Factory Brand
- Famous Brand
- Fashion Shoes
- Jarman Shoes
- Liz Claiborne
- Marty's
- Rack Room Shoes
- Red Wing Shoes
- SAS Shoes
- Taha Shoes Outlet
- Tanger Outlet
- Two Lips Shoes

These are just *some* of the outlets you can search for great buys on brand-name and new discovery shoes. I say "new discovery" shoes because you might just discover a non-brand-name shoe line that fits beautifully, looks expensive, and is fine on the wallet.

And don't forget that outlet stores have *sales*, too. Sixty-five percent off plus another 20 percent off? Again, a huge shoe victory. Check their websites or call the stores to find out when they have their seasonal sales, and—very important—be aware that *their* idea of end-of-summer might be very different from your calendar expectations. Stores like to push us to the next holiday, so that end-of-summer shoe sale could take place in May. If you wait until July, you might be surrounded by Uggs and shiny plastic snowboots at that outlet. You've missed it. Always make the call.

Your Favorite Clothing Stores

They're not department stores, but they might be right next to one in the mall. I'm talking about stores like Ann Taylor and Ann Taylor Loft, where their Celebrations shoes are often marked down from $188 to $49 or less. And if your dresses came from Ann Taylor, you could get that color-match without the whole dyeing thing. For my wedding, my girls were in sage Ann Taylor Celebrations dresses with the matching sage green shoes. They looked divine, and so did the price tag. We watched the site together, waiting for that red sale number to show up under the shoes that went with the dress, and scooped them up for more than $50 off!

At the website for Newport News, I scouted out elegant satin pumps in black, silver, and the new trendy neutrals for $49, down from $64. For the same price, I spotted satin d'orsay pumps with rhinestone accents. And I then clicked on the SALE button to discover $19 simple silver slingbacks. "If you're not crazy about the dresses in some catalogs," suggests one bridesmaid from Nashville, "their shoes could still be a fabulous find!"

Don't count out casual clothing stores like Banana Republic, The Limited, Annie Sez, and other shops, where you can find lovely strappy heels for under $30. And perhaps for less when you scout out a coupon to any of these stores at RetailMeNot.com or any of the other coupon sites listed in the Resources section of this book.

Discount Shoe Stores

Here's where we get to the Payless racks, as well as those at DSW and MJM, and other discount shoe store chains in your region. During a recent visit to DSW, I had to give my wallet to my husband so that I *didn't* go wild with their $29 shoe sale on pretty strappy heels from the top shoe brands:

- Ann Marino
- BCBG
- Caparro's
- Ellen Tracy
- Jessica Simpson
- Jones New York
- JS
- Madden Girl
- Moda
- Unlisted
- And more . . .

If you have a membership card to this discount shoe store, you can get extra discounts automatically applied or coupons emailed to you on a regular basis, or this shoe purchase can be stamped on your Buy 5, Get One Free card for your future shoe buys.

And It Gets Even Better . . .

Don't forget that DSW and others like it have their own websites, often with free shipping when you spend $30 or more.

I've seen magnificent sales in shopping centers near casinos, believe it or not. That's where a great many outlet and discount stores are popping up, enticing those slot machine winners to drop their newfound cash on a great pair of BCBG heels. So the next time you're vacationing at or driving past a casino area, stop in at the shoe shops and potentially score your low-cost wedding shoes.

Now's a good time to talk about location. Shoes are usually going to be more expensive when you're shopping in a major metropolitan city than when you're shopping in your suburban town, or in a *college* town. That's right. College students need shoes, too, and the stores near them price to sell. So if you can get to a university town, look for some shoe stores in the area. You'll be floored by the price differentials. When I recently visited the campus of the University of North Carolina, I almost fell over when I saw some clothing and shoe prices as compared to the shops in my northeastern hometown. We're talking 40 percent less for the same designer brands and styles I saw back home.

Bridal Dress Web Sites

When your group is about to select dresses from a bridal designer website, check to see if they offer a percentage off on shoes for your group. I looked at Dessy's website and found adorable ballet flats for just $28, and you can get them in colors to match twenty-four of the company's dress shades. At David's Bridal, ballet flats were $39 and dyeable. (We'll get into the dyeable issue later in this chapter!)

Watch Out for Outdated Recommendations!

On many bridal websites, you'll see suggestions to shop at specialty bridal shoe sites, but keep in mind that some sites have had their articles online for *years*. Sometimes a site that had great deals ten years ago isn't the most budget-priced anymore. And some point you to pricey sites. I visited MyGlassSlipper.com recently and was astounded at some of the pricey shoes on there (albeit listed with a few budget-priced shoe styles). The $10 dye offer sounds great, but if the shoes are over $200 . . . not so fabulous. So always look closely at any bridal site's link to a shoe source, because it might be outdone by a newer shoe source.

Bridal Shops

There are two kinds: the full-service bridal shop the bride shops at—with a sizeable rack of bridesmaid gowns, shoes, and accessories—and bridesmaid-specific stores that only stock and sell to the bridesmaids. Treat them both equally, and you may be able to take advantage of great price breaks.

The first may be found in the bride's shop. When she buys her dress there, all of her bridesmaids can receive 10 to 20 percent off their dress *and* shoe purchases at the same shop. Depending on the salon's prices—since some can be quite upscale and overpriced—this may compute to a great bargain on the perfect pair of shoes. Granted, bridal shops often have inflated prices on shoes and accessories, so put your comparison shopping skills to work, counting this source as just one of your possibilities.

The second applies to both types of shops, and you already know about this step from the dresses chapter: Get on the shop's mailing list to receive advance-notice, VIP invitations to upcoming, unadvertised *trunk sales*, which can net you up to 80 percent off your wedding day shoes and accessories. Yes, again, you're going to get lots of junk mail from the shops and their partners, but I'd rather spend a few minutes hitting DELETE in order to net 80 percent off a great pair of designer shoes that look amazing with the dress!

Trunk sales are a bridesmaid's dream come true, since you might get top-name designer shoes for a steal. Keep in mind, though, that it's going to be the sizes they have on hand that you'll shop from. They don't order and mail to you. So if you have a tiny foot, such as size 5, or a larger foot, your odds might be slimmer than if you're a 7. But you never know. These sales are meant to unload a designer's outgoing collection, so maybe there will be *lots* of size 5s and 5.5s in the displays. But here's a little secret: Since the 7s get snapped up, ask the trunk sale director if the designer has extra 5s to unload. You might be able to arrange to buy your pair for 80 percent off and have the shoes shipped to the salon for you.

Wedding Blogs

Follow the top budget wedding blogs, like BrokeAssBride.com, to find out about smartly priced shoes and accessories, and also get the editor's scoop on the hottest shoe sales going on right now. Some bridal blogs even offer a special coupon discount of 20 percent or more when you mention that you learned about the sale from them!

eBay

Louboutins for $45. You'll find them on eBay. I've found them. I wear them. Shop smartly, and you'll find a wealth of *new*, boxed designer shoes that have been listed there by bridal gown shop owners who don't want to hold trunk sales, as well as by shoe stores that want an easy way to unload their merchandise. Knowing that so many women buy their special occasion heels online, more wedding industry vendors are placing their shoe stock on the site . . . and you score huge bargains. Again, shop smartly. Because not every listed Louboutin is a real one. I'm just sayin'.

And be sure to review both the Auctions Only listings as well as the Buy It Now shoe auctions to net the best bargain price. As mentioned earlier, eBay has trended toward the Buy It Now option more and more lately, which might keep you from winning a $20 pair of heels, so explore the offerings with smart shopping tactics.

Online Shoe Sources

In the Resources section of this book, you'll find a list of online shoe sources, many of which you might already know. Zappo's, for instance, is one of the most popular online shoe and handbag resources, with its collection of big-name and mid-name designers and discount prices. I've had a lot of luck at Overstock.com, nabbing some gorgeous heels to wear to weddings . . . all for over 35 percent off.

One amazing new resource I found is MyShoes.com, which takes your shoe search details—style, heel height, features such as ankle straps or bows, color, and price range—and delivers instant finds from hundreds of retailers. And they throw in coupon codes that they find for you at PromotionalCodes.com, saving you an additional percent off and perhaps free shipping. I hunted on the site and found gorgeous silver slingbacks for $34 and Jessica Simpson Collection heels in the $30 range, as well. This site is going to save you a ton of time, and deliver fantastic discount finds.

Just One Google Away

Don't forget that the online shoe sources, including department stores and discount shoe store websites, often offer significant percentages off in their seasonal sales. All you have to do to get *even more money off* is to Google for discount codes and check your new faves RetailMeNot.com and PromotionalCodes.com to cash in on big, big discounts and free shipping deals. And since coupons are in demand these days, most reliable shopping sites offer them readily. You just have to look, or sign up for each store's e-newsletter to be alerted to their one-day-only, member, VIP, holiday, and weekend sales.

No matter where you're looking, bargain shopping is always a timing game. Different discounts pop up at different times, depending on the shoes that hit the "conveyor belt" leading them to discount sellers (and to your closet!). So don't buy the first discounted pair of shoes that you find, unless it's a mega-discount for fabulous shoes and your gut is telling you to go for it.

DIY Shoe Dress-Up

Our sisters in the DIY Bridesmaid Brigade like to take a simple, inexpensive shoe and dress it up a little bit … just like the bride does. Budget-challenged brides are using these tips to turn a $20 pair of shoes into a pretty style that looks far pricier:

• Attaching jeweled clips to their simple, white satin shoes to give the appearance of a sparkling, expensive, designer shoe for one-tenth the price. Find these jeweled shoe accents at department stores, on eBay and Etsy, and—for free—borrow them from friends who did the same with their shoes.

• Adding *floral* clips. A $19 simple strappy heel can—with the addition of even a tiny floral clip instead of a gemstone accent—look like it cost over $75. Check out the shoe sources and the wedding website resources at the end of this book to discover your ideal shoe clip-ons.

• Visiting teen accessory stores at the mall. Claire's and other bright and colorful teen accessory chains are hotbeds of inexpensive, clip-on shoe accents with shine, color, and sparkle, and given that *Teen Vogue* shows some pretty sophisticated accessory styles right now, it's not the center of the Hello Kitty universe. There's some fabulous stuff in there!

• Visiting the craft store for everything you need to make your shoe clip-ons for under $10—gemstones, clip kits, the glue, and sealant. And a free weekend class to teach you how to do it. Nice.

TO DYE OR NOT TO DYE

Earlier in this chapter, I mentioned bridesmaid shoes dyed to match the salmon- or lavender-hued dress. While many brides are opting to skip the shoe dye hassle and expense in favor of asking bridesmaids to wear their own choice of strappy silver heels, you might have a bride who really wants your shoes to match the dress.

So, to find inexpensive shoes and make the dye process more affordable, keep in mind that Payless has a line of discount dyeable shoes, that you'll find dyeable shoes at many department stores, that MyShoes.com lets you shop for dyeables in your price range (I found a fabulous pair for under $40!), and that you'll also find budget-friendly styles at these websites:

- www.discountweddingshoes.com
- www.dyeables.com
- www.dyeableshoesonline.com
- www.dyeableshoestore.com
- www.shoestomatch.com

(I haven't shopped at these sites, so I'm not endorsing them—just letting you know they're there.)

In addition to the expense of buying and dyeing your shoes, you'll face the essential task of having all of the bridesmaids' shoes ordered and dyed in one lot, so that the shade matches exactly. So the maid of honor gets to run the task of collecting everyone's sizes, collect their payments, and even arrange to ship the shoes to the bridesmaids so that they can wear them to their dress fittings. (Be warned! For one reason or another, this task might fall to *you*!) It's a lot of extra work, but if this is the plan for your group, be prepared to send a check that includes extra amounts for shipping and insurance.

And of course, if you wish to avoid the shoe-dye hassles, the top shoe colors that work with most dress hues are: silver and gold, and also nude or neutral shades that are easily located in your budget shoe search.

JEWELRY

Some brides choose to give their bridesmaids necklace and earring sets to coordinate with their wedding-day dresses as their thank-you gifts, and some simply instruct their bridesmaids to wear jewelry of their own. The request might be to wear a silver necklace and silver dangle earrings with no color, or even pearl strands and pearl stud earrings. Faux pearl is fine. It all depends on how detailed the bride's vision is as far as your accessories. Very few brides are going to send you a link to a $40 necklace and tell you to order one of these, too.

What Not to Google

I wouldn't search online for "discount bridesmaid jewelry," since you're going to be led to a mountain of bridal websites offering the same or similar-looking gemstone necklaces and earrings selling for twice what you'd pay at Target, Kohls, Marshalls, or other divine discount stores. Just because it says "discount" doesn't always make it the best deal possible, not even at big-name bridal websites. I took a quick look through one of the biggest bridal sites out there and found bridesmaid jewelry selling at over $20 per set, plus shipping. You can do better.

So your budget brilliance here is in finding a pretty necklace, earrings, and perhaps a bracelet that works perfectly with your dress and your dollar figures. Here are my suggestions to help you save:

• I'm a huge fan of Target for this. Their silver jewelry is so varied and so classic, most often priced in the $6 to $15 range per piece. And these simple silver hoops, dangles, pendant necklaces, and even faux pearl studs are definitely something you can wear again. Shop Walmart, Kohls, Marshalls, and other similar well-priced stores to score your inexpensive, pretty jewelry, as well.

• Steer clear of bridal shops for your coordinated jewelry pieces. Even at sale prices, they're often priced for impulse-buying by the very excited bride and her equally enthused bridesmaids who fall in love with a $50 Akoya pearls set.

• Shop the racks at teen accessories stores like Claire's for a great selection of simple silver dangles or stylish colored jewelry sets.

• Believe it or not, street fairs and festivals are great places to find $5 necklace and earrings sets to coordinate with the bridesmaid jewelry style.

DIY Jewelry

More bridesmaids are saving money by making their own jewelry, often at craft parties the bride and the bridesmaids plan together, where you all share the goods from someone's jewelry-making kit, customizing your own silver pendant necklace, or wiring your own detailed gemstone necklaces and dangle earrings. The kits you'll find at craft stores are inexpensive, and you'll often find there a *wall* of pendants, gemstone pieces, and other fresh-looking, stylish jewelry pieces. And even a free class on how to make your own jewelry … which many a bridesmaid has fallen in love with and turned into a sideline career.

Watch Out!

When it comes to jewelry, I'm a fan of buying on-site, not *through* a site, to avoid shipping charges, which can be almost the same cost as the item itself!

Speaking of DIY jewelry, you might think that Etsy.com is a great place to find handmade jewelry, but I must warn you that prices vary like wild on this site. Some artisans charge inflated prices to cover their costs and give themselves a dash of upper-echelon *status*, as in, "My line is so hot, I can charge $50 per necklace." Granted, some artists are using great quality silver and gemstones and imported ceramic beads, and perhaps their prices are justified. But there's often the extra expense of shipping that tacks on an extra 10 percent or more to the price, which surprises bridesmaids upon checkout.

BRAS AND UNDERGARMENTS

Ask any gown designer or alterations professional, and he or she will tell you that a fabulous supportive bra and seamless slimmers beneath your dress are the most essential accessories for your gorgeous wedding day look. You could have the prettiest hot-designer earrings on, but if The Girls are not up where they should be, or if you have back bra bulge, *that's* what stands out, what your image will scream to the room as your first (and only) impression. So move "get a better bra" and "get a sleek slimmer" to the top of your to-do list, and be cheered: You won't have to spend top-dollar on brand-name undergarments and beautiful bras that—when chosen well—can give the impression of taking ten pounds off of your silhouette and give you that celeb-style you envy on the covers of your favorite fashion magazines.

A great bra is the best thing you can do for how you look in your bridesmaid dress. And a great slimmer can pull in that tummy pooch. The keyword is *great*. And *great* is out there at bargain prices. I did a bit of reconnaissance to find the best-priced Wonderbra during one particular week in March—during prom time and right before wedding season when prices were only a little bit inflated. Here's what I found during just an hour of clicking around on my computer:

Wonderbra: Full Foam Padding, strapless

- *Macys: $34*

- *Nordstrom: $38–$76*

- *eBay:* NEW, packaged: $8.99 on auction's first day; corset version was $9.99 at auction

- *Amazon.com:* Yes, they have new bras on Amazon! *$17-$34*

- *Spanx: $62*

- *OneHanesPlace.com: $22.99, in a range of colors and styles, in foam pushup and underwire*

- *Victoria's Secret:* Full-priced, not during a bra sale event, *$45-$58*

I decided to put my coupon code savvy into action, clicked onto RetailMeNot.com, and was delivered *with a 10 percent off coupon code* to a site I'd never heard of, LeadApparel.com, which had Wonderbras priced at $26.95.

Keep an eye out for department store sales and VictoriasSecret.com bra sale events, at which you can purchase fabulous, top-quality bras for up to 60 percent off. And there's nothing better than putting on a fresh, new bra and seeing how much better you look in the mirror!

Shop the Bra Sites

Check out the bargain prices for top-name brand bras at:

- BareNecessities.com
- Hanes.com
- BraStop.com
- OneHanesPlace.com

Slimmers

Just like with your bra, as well as with your shoes and all of the elements of your look that have to deliver *quality*, it's worth it to spend a little more and not take that lowest-of-the-low price on a random brand. Spanx has become the industry standard for slimmers in both panties style and in the longer versions that slim your hips and thighs. Style experts say that designs that begin right under your bra line smooth your tummy and prevent that horrific "roll" that cheaper brands can descend to right at your waistline.

So I explored the Spanx website and found fabulous slimmers in the $53 range, with lower prices offered in their sales and with an online coupon code. So it's perfectly reasonable to expect to land a $40 or so slimmer that will take a few inches off your frame. At Victoria's Secret, slimmers ranged from $28 to $42.

I also found terrific, budget-priced slimmers at Target, in the ASSETS by Sara Blakely line, at just $14 to $16 for the panties design and $28 for the thigh-shaper, and while it doesn't pull in the tummy to the same degree as full-on Spanx, it creates a sleek, flattering effect. This line also provides slimming stockings at $12 to $16.

Speaking of stockings, Wolford brand hose are considered among the top brands for their indulgent fabrics and super strength, and I landed several pairs of brand-new, still-packaged stockings at less than half-price on eBay. Donna Karan brand stockings are also among my picks for best support and style, and at department stores, these were retail priced at $18. On eBay, I found new, packaged Donna Karan stockings available for $5.99. So while you *could* pick up a $4 pair of stockings at the supermarket's display case—if you think a stocking is a stocking is a stocking—I love this one as a little bit of indulgence you can get yourself for the wedding day and afterward. Especially when you use the Department Store Sale + Store/Online Coupon formula to remove 30 percent or more from the price.

From bras to slimmers to stockings, an investment of $50 or so can create a *priceless* thrill when you try on that bridesmaid dress and *love* how much better, thinner, and sexier you look than if you tried to save a few bucks and just wear your own, tired, less-supportive bra and depend on a basic control-top pantyhose that you've pulled from the clump of already-worn stockings in your underwear drawer.

WRAPS AND OTHER ACCESSORIES

"I wanted to give my bridesmaids a thank-you gift they'd use again in the future and that would coordinate them on the wedding day without them spending extra money," says one bride from Tampa. "So I got them all pretty pashmina wraps for my winter wedding. I went with white, knowing that would be far better for them than a blue or a pink—it's tough to fit everyone's jacket colors—and they wound up wearing their wraps in church, where we found out that the house of worship required women to have their shoulders covered. So it worked out perfectly."

Wraps, pashminas and jackets are increasingly chosen to give the bridesmaids' dresses a more demure look for the ceremony, and then everyone can remove them to reveal the strapless looks for the reception. Many bridesmaids say they get a lot more use out of a pretty wrap than they do the jewelry given to them by the bride.

Which is great to know *if the bride is giving you a wrap.*

But many don't. They just leave it to you to plan for your own wrap or jacket to guard against a winter wedding or spring evening chill. As charming as it is when your date drapes his jacket over your shoulders, it's better for you to plan your own stylish wrap or jacket purchase. Especially if you'll be at an outdoor, beach, boat, spring, late fall, or winter wedding.

In the past, budget articles told you to avoid bridal websites, but I found some fantastic deals on matching pashminas at the bridal gown sources. At Dessy, for instance, their *matching* pashminas were just $32, and they also provide matching $22 clutches and $9 headbands in twenty four of their dress shades. So if the bride loves the matchy-matchy look, your accessories can oblige at prices that save all of the bridesmaids money.

Department stores have vast lines of pretty pashminas and wonderful wraps, and there are several times in the year when you'll find these accessories on sale:

• Pre-winter sales: Starting in late September, department stores try to entice your purchase with attractive 20 percent off sales.

• Post-holiday sales: Since department stores operate on different calendar holiday timing than we do, post-holiday sales often occur right on the holiday, or slightly before. Gotta get these winter dresses and accessories out of the store by December to make room for spring clothes and island vacation clothing! So December to January often lines up great sales.

• Prom time: Even high school girls accessorize with pretty chiffon scarves and tassled-edge wraps, so hit the prom collections starting in . . . get this . . . February. And if you don't score a low-cost wrap, come back in late April to select from the on-sale collections of wraps, scarves, bolero jackets, and other current styles of cover-ups.

• Easter sales. That's also February, in the women's department.

• eBay. Look for NWT—"new with tags"—or "Gently Worn" wraps that you can get for less than $5.

If the Bride Wants You in Gloves

If the bride wants the bridesmaids in gloves to suit her ultra-formal wedding, you can save a bundle by skipping the gloves shown in the bridal shop display case—which are often price-elevated—and shop instead on websites featuring gloves for debutante balls and pageants. I visited a pageant gown site and found pretty, elbow-length gloves in every color from sky blue to tangerine and deeper jewel shades of cobalt blue and purple available for $13.95. On a bridal website, I saw long gloves priced at $30. It's an ugly truth in a beautiful world: Whenever an item is marked as "bridal," the price is usually marked higher. So explore prom gown, pageant, and debutante accessory sites wisely, and you could make the bride's wish for all-formal-gloved bridesmaids come true *and* be the budget hero for the rest of the bridesmaids when you report that you can get the gloves for $8 per pair, group discount landed.

Or, suggest that the bride may want to stand out as the only one wearing ultra-formal gloves, while you and the brides-maids carry the formality in your dress, hairstyle, and accessories.

If department store prices are too steep for you, here's an easy solution: Make your own wrap! Or, if one of the bridesmaids is—or you are—handy with a sewing machine and basic hemming skills, the bridal party members' wraps can be easily made using fabric bought at a discount fabric store. A talented DIY friend can even sew in those beaded edges and stylish tassel ends. Of course, your chosen crafter has to be really gifted, since a messy hem ruins the effect.

CHAPTER 7

Beauty Expenses

*T*he average expense of a bride's beauty treatments—having her hair, makeup, and nails professionally done as part of the group that goes to the spa or salon on the wedding morning—is over $140. TheWeddingReport.com's survey says bridesmaids are spending $65 on their hairstyle, $32 on their manicure, and $30 on their pedicure. Plus tips, which, if you're a "good tipper," can add another $20 to $40 to your tally. And that's not the end of the beauty expenses that many bridesmaids face!

Whether encouraged (or demanded) by the bride, some bridesmaids join her in signing up for gym memberships, boot camps, and other get-in-shape-for-the-big-day programs. And some decide that the bride is not the only one who needs to look great in person and in photos, so they embark upon professional tanning treatments, waxing, even professional or self-done teeth whitening regimens to stand out in that circle of pretty bridesmaids.

Before we get into the budget-saving strategies for the Big Three of bridesmaids beauty—hair, makeup, and nails—and the additional beauty steps you might be preparing to take, let's first cover a very big topic: whether or not the bride will pick up your tab for the wedding-day salon visit or the stylist's on-site visit to glam you all up.

True, some brides have the extra funds to pay for your and the other bridesmaids' hair, makeup, and mani-pedis, so their girls are off the hook. These indulgent treatments during the group outing to the spa or salon may be the bride's *thank-you gift* to the bridesmaids. But unless the bride has said *recently* that this will be the case, that you won't be responsible for your beauty tab, don't assume she's paying the bill. I've heard from plenty of bridesmaids whose own circle of friends regularly pick up the beauty bill as How It's Done, and then they're shocked and offended when the bride asks them for their $140 share. Plus tips. Making that assumption is a very, very big mistake.

You'll notice that I said *recently* when it comes to the bride's offer to pay. That's because the bride might have offered *months ago*, right after she became engaged and when she invited you to be in the bridal party and offered to "cover your expenses." But that was said before the bills started rolling in for the wedding plans. Now, she might not be able to pay for your beauty expenses, and she might not even remember offering.

So it's best to ask her what the prices are, or if she can direct you to the salon's website so that you can check the price lists. If she *does* plan to pay for your hair, makeup, and nails—or perhaps just your hair, if that's all she expects her bridesmaids to have done—this is when she'll tell you not to worry about it, that the trip to the salon is on her. If she doesn't, or can't keep that original promise, this is where she tells you she's arranged for a group discount, or that the package she booked with the salon gets you all 20 percent off. And that there will be a breakfast buffet and champagne at the salon for her group's VIP treatment.

WHAT DOES THE BRIDE WANT FOR YOUR HAIR?

Before you panic about another $150 flying out of your wallet, keep this in mind: It's a growing trend for brides to allow their bridesmaids to do their own hair, makeup, and nails. The fabulous bride knows that she's expecting a lot of cash outlay from her bridesmaids, so she gives her girls a break and lets everyone glam up on their own.

"I love the look of the sleek, simple low ponytail with a jeweled clip for my bridesmaids," says one soon-to-be-bride. "And it doesn't take a professional stylist to flatiron, brush back, and clip hair into that look." If the bride wants you all in curly updos, that, too, is an easily DIY'd look created with a spritz of volumizing spray, a swept-up clip, and a group share of a ceramic-plated barrel curling iron.

Freebie Spirals and Flowing Waves

Call it a great reason to get together for a bridesmaids' party. You bring your fabulous spiral-maker curling iron, and someone else brings the hummus and pita chips. Uncork the wine, and you have a girls' hairstyle try-out session, during which you practice creating curly updos or heat up those hot rollers to show the bride what you, or a member of your group, can create for all the bridesmaids' wedding day look. Just like the bride wants to see how the gowns will look on you, she'll enjoy and appreciate that you're giving her the chance to see and suggest the different types of hairstyles her bridesmaids may wear. There are so many "How to Create an Updo" articles—particularly on About.com—and even video lessons on YouTube, it's easy to find a do-able 'do that lets you save a lot of money.

Another option that's growing in popularity: A friend who *is* a hairstylist—whether she's in the bridal party or not—can volunteer to style everyone's hair, including the bride's, *as her wedding gift*. The "My Services in Trade As a Gift" trend is picking up speed as more wedding guests are eager to help the bride create her dream day and avoid having to give a $300 or more cash wedding gift on the big day. With this talented stylist friend doing everyone's hair on the wedding morning, her time is worth money, which creates a win-win situation. Perhaps eight or more win-wins when she saves each bridesmaid that $65 or more!

How do you make this scenario a reality? Simply suggest it to the maid of honor or directly to the bride: "I know that Lisa's a really talented hair stylist, and she does a lot of wedding hairstyles at the salon where she works. What would you think about having her do the bridesmaids' hair?" The bride may *love* this idea, since she may have been dreading having to ask you all to shell out hairstyle money. It's something for her to consider, and to follow up on if she so chooses, unless she asks you to take on this helpful task for her.

The Most Unexpected Stylist

"Believe it or not, I found out that my *junior bridesmaid* learned how to French braid hair during her months as a summer camp counselor, and she really perfected the art of the modern braid like I've seen in *InStyle* and on Jennifer Aniston lately. So I asked her if she'd be willing to braid the four bridesmaids' hair on the wedding day, and she was *so* excited that there was something she could contribute! Everyone looked amazing, and they treated my junior bridesmaid like a celebrity stylist with the compliments and telling other people that she did their hair. She was *so* proud of herself!"

—SARAH, RECENT BRIDE

If the bride is one of those who wants her bridesmaids to have matching hairstyles that require extensions, point out to her that the fine-quality clip-in ponytails, curly puffs, and length extensions at HairUWear.com will do the job perfectly, for far less than a professional salon process that can cost hundreds of dollars. You'll see the Jessica Simpson line of HairDo clip-ins at that site for under $40 a kit. And a stylist can even help you color-match your shade. Plus, you get to reuse those cute ponies and puffs in the future.

Watch Out for Your Own DIY Disasters

Brides are warned not to do it, and so, too, do you need to be extra-cautious when it comes to trying to save money by dyeing or highlighting your own hair. It's a fine money-saving idea *if you've always dyed or highlighted your own hair*. If you know that the Ginger Spice shade of Garnier Nutrisse delivers perfect color and softness for your hair, and you've been coloring your own hair for years, then go for it.

But now is not the time to say, "Eight dollars for a box of dye versus $60 for a professional dye job at a salon? I think I'll try dyeing my own hair." Because a bad dye job or fried ends or patches of missed color is not the look you're going for on the bride and groom's big day. If you're a newbie to the hair color and highlight arena, have a pro create your best shade, highlights, and lowlights, because messing up your hair is going to cost a lot more than if you had a pro do it in the first place.

Time It to Save

Schedule your pre-wedding haircuts and colors to meet your *regularly scheduled* hair appointments, which means you spend no extra money for an additional visit to the salon.

MAKEUP SOLUTIONS

The bride might have arranged for a group rate at the bridal salon or with her on-site makeup artist as part of the bridal package she's booked, so that your professional makeup application might cost you only a nominal amount. Perhaps 20 percent off.

Or, the bride might follow the advice that's currently being pushed to her by countless bridal websites and allow you to do your own makeup.

This is one area where you really can't tell the bride you prefer to opt out of the professional makeup application, since that's in the realm of being a Troublemaker Bridesmaid. If she wants you to get the pro treatment, budget your bridesmaid funds and play nice with the group. This part of the wedding morning preparations is a fabulous way to relax and enjoy the excitement with the other bridesmaids who get their makeovers, marveling at the way their eyecolor now pops and their foundation looks amazing.

If the bride does entrust your own makeup application to you, put in some extra effort in exchange for the freebie to explore pretty makeup shades suggested to you *for free* at the department store makeup counter, where you shouldn't feel pressured to buy any product you aren't absolutely in love with. For many bridesmaids, this freebie consultation is priceless when they see that a plum-colored eyeliner brings out their brown eyes so much better than the brown liner they've been wearing, and they learn the *right* way to pencil in and perfect their brows. Your $25 investment in a light-reflecting foundation and powder could result in what *looks* like a $100 makeup application.

A perk of this research visit to the makeup counter is that you may improve your look for your everyday beauty, not just for the wedding day.

Buying New Makeup

You may be used to your everyday neutrals, or to your eye-catching bright liner, but now might be the time to freshen your cosmetics with new shades, and with an improved formula of mascara. Shop the beauty supply stores rather than department stores to net big savings of 30 percent or more on top-name brands, and check out the discounts and sales at Drugstore.com when you know the brand and color name of the foundation, eye, or lip makeup you'll wear. I've also found great makeup sales at Target and Walmart.

MANI-PEDIS

The trend today is for the bridesmaids to do their own nails, with the bride directing the color and style for that matching, uniform look. So you might be asked to wear a French manicure, or the maid of honor might email you with a note saying to use Cotton Candy by Essie. Ask ahead of time if the bridesmaids are going to be getting mani-pedis at the morning-of salon visit, since some brides are too busy to send out a note on that topic. You don't want to be the only one showing up with undone nails, needing to sit down with a manicurist on your dime while everyone else is on-schedule with their hair and makeup. That's $30 or more down the tubes, and you'd be that Troublemaker Bridesmaid who throws off the clockwork itinerary for the group beauty treatments.

BRIDESMAID BOOT CAMP?

A recent episode of *Bridezillas* featured a bride who required her brides-maids to sign up for a pricey boot camp months before the wedding, "so that all of my bridesmaids will look great in their gowns." That example of selfishness might have landed her a spot on a reality show and a guest segment on a morning talk show (during which she didn't realize the hosts were pointing out the rudeness of her demands), but it didn't earn her any love from her circle of bridesmaids. I'm sure your bride isn't this egomaniacal, but yours *might* ask you to sign up for a fitness class with her as her motivation buddy. She might even think that having her bridesmaids sign up for classes with her will provide for the girls' time she doesn't otherwise have in her busy schedule.

If you have the available funds and would enjoy getting up at 6 a.m. to do push-ups in a parking lot, or going after work to take a pole-dancing class, then go for it!

Otherwise, it's fine to mention to the bride that while you'd love to join her, you have neither the money nor the time to commit to boot camp, twelve weeks of nonrefundable yoga classes, or membership to a gym. What you *can* do, and would love to do *with* her, is plan the occasional get-together for tennis or hiking or biking—all free at your neighborhood park or trails. Your Sunday morning get-togethers then provide your burst of fitness, and the chance to spend some friend-time together in a relaxed atmosphere that allows you to *talk*. (They frown on that at boot camp or yoga class.)

If you or another bridesmaid has a home gym, or that collection of fitness equipment in the spare room or basement, then perhaps you can arrange a stop-by on the weekends to hop on that recumbent while she's on the elliptical and again, chat about the latest news and catch up on the things you used to talk about before the wedding season became the Big Topic. The bride needs a break from all that wedding talk to keep her sanity, and you, too, would love to experience the return of your friend, the bride.

One big trend is plugging in the Wii Fit your boyfriend or little brother has at the house and laugh with the bride as you virtually box one another, snowboard, or bowl. And if you or another bridesmaid lives in a community with a pool, it's time for water aerobics, water volleyball, or swimming laps. Your neighborhood park may have a basketball court for a fun game of H-O-R-S-E, and community trails may have workout stations where you can do pull-ups and sit-ups as you make your way through the miles of gorgeous scenery.

And of course, if it's your goal to lose some weight and tone up for the wedding day, all of these fitness ideas are yours to use solo or with your sweetie. Move that exercise bike into the living room so you can ride while you watch television. Keep a set of hand weights by the couch so you can do biceps curls during commercials. And bridesmaids say they're borrowing each other's fitness DVDs to keep variety in their workout regimens for free. The library also has a stack of fresh workout DVDs to check out, and if you have a dog who needs daily walking, there's your no-cost workout that's great for both of you.

Freebie Fitness Sites

Check out these websites for additional free motivation and tracking as you work toward your own health and fitness goals:

- SparkPeople.com: Workout videos and a personalized fitness plan by experts for you

- FitDay.com: Charts that track your calories eaten versus burned

- WeightLossBuddy.com: Diet friends to motivate and check in with, plus nutritionist advice

Check out your cable company's On Demand offerings, which allow you to click on *free* workouts in cardio, toning, yoga, and even trendy workouts like urban hip-hop and stripperobics. Right now, my cable company is offering an extensive series of workouts by *Buff Bride* celebrity expert (and former trainer to Katie Holmes) Sue Fleming, so I get to tone my back, butt, arms, core, and legs for *free* every morning.

Part Two

Showers and Parties

CHAPTER 8

Planning the Bridal Shower—The Basics

*T*he prospect of planning a bridal shower can be extremely daunting, especially when you look at the huge amounts that some bridesmaids have had to pay for shower plans that spun out of control ($700 to $900 apiece in some cases!), and even for modestly planned showers that still added up to more than a bridesmaid could comfortably spend. Here's where you'll help your group gravitate toward smarter, more budget-friendly bridal shower *basics* that save tons of money and still allow you to have a blast planning a creative, fabulous celebration for the bride (and groom, if it will be a coed shower)!

Following these guidelines can save you *50 percent or more* on your grand total, and with the many freebies and DIYs you can add to the mix, you're on your way to planning the best bridal shower ever . . . that *no one* will be able to tell is actually a budget party. Read on, and get excited again about co-planning the celebration. . . .

WHO'S ON THE PLANNING TEAM?

In years past, the maid of honor was the Party Chief, and the bridesmaids were the decision- and cost-sharing co-planners. Every expense was split four ways or more, which made the average bridesmaid's share of the catering, cake, drinks, décor, and more about 20 percent of the tally. Not bad.

But *now*, in our financially challenged era, it's becoming quite common for *additional people* to join in the shower-planning group. We're talking moms, stepmoms, grandmothers, multiple parents on each side, godmothers, and in some cultures the bride's "sponsor" or mentor wife who is named as the bride's chief advisor on all things wifely. So the circle of planning hosts may be much larger, perhaps ten people or more, which makes your share of the budget tally *10 percent*.

Yes, there's a trade-off to having lots of planners involved, and you may *earn* that extra 10 percent off when the door has been opened to an opinionated mom or a grandmother who insists upon a more elaborate menu. But that's the way it goes, and it's up to the maid of honor to corral those who might add extra expenses to the shower plans, to keep prices down, and to gently remind moms and grandmoms that they're part of a team, not in the lead.

Still, if the topic arises of inviting moms and others to join your planning ranks, remind the mulling-it-over bridesmaids that the planning season will be quite short, and that not every mom is going to be a powermonger. If the maid of honor is nervous about being placed in a position of having to say no to the mom—perhaps it's *her* mom—suggest that you discuss as a group of bridesmaids *how* you will arrange to work with the moms, how the maid of honor can deliver a polite and diplomatic no when the mom emails with yet another pricey addition to the party plans. I suggest this script:

> (Mom's name), thank you for suggesting such a lovely
> idea for the shower. It does, however, push us above our budget,
> so this is one of those fantastic ideas that we can't use for the shower,
> but we hope you'll use it for some part of the wedding weekend,
> such as your morning-after breakfast. (Bride and groom)
> will love it! It's just beyond our theme and the plans we already
> have set! Thanks for sending, and I look forward to seeing
> you at the planning dinner next week!

This message is filled with lots of compliments the mom will love, and she might respond with her offer to pay for the entire extra station or the larger, more elaborate cake she has in mind. If so, that may be great news for your group! That station and that cake now become *free* to you, and mom gets to bring her idea into the celebration.

Understanding Mom

Don't look at the moms as Evil Corruptors of your budget. Most often, they're just looking for ways to make things extra-nice for the bride and groom, and yes, there may be a little bit of ego and showing-off involved. With more moms bumped out of planning the wedding itself, they get their planning buzz from helping to plan the bridal shower. So if you have a plan-increasing mom on your hands, pre-plan with the other bridesmaids about how you'll handle it if the mom wants to insert her ideas *and pay for them*. And pre-plan how you'll say a polite and self-respecting no if she insists that the group can split the costs of her inspirations. Mom doesn't want to be The Outsider. She wants *some* parts of the day to stand out as her contributions. That's perfectly understandable. Mom just wants to enjoy this, too.

And then there's the wedding coordinator. Yes, some maids of honor and bridesmaids think just like the bride—maybe having *been* brides before, and knowing how fabulous a job pro planners do in organizing plans and creating a fabulous budget celebration—and choose to hire an expert to suggest low-cost, impressive sites and excellent caterers whose price sheets save money. Visit www.bridalassn.com to find a fabulous, local coordinator through the Association of Bridal Consultants, interview them as a group to see if you like their vibe as well as their portfolio, and talk specifically about how he or she will keep you on your budget while still arranging the special party elements you desire. A great planner can show you budget spreadsheets from events she's planned before, pointing out the free cake she negotiated for this bridal party, and the bump-up to a top-shelf bar she negotiated for that bridal party.

With a professional on your team, you can get better local savings than you would have found on your own, *and* you get an experienced mediator to deliver that "thanks, but no thanks" speech to the pushy mom. "*That* was awesome! For just a few hundred dollars, we got a planner who saved us twice that on our upscale bridal shower plans, *and* she was so fabulous in talking down the bride's mom, preventing us from having to pay a fortune for all the extra stuff her mom wanted to add. *And* none of us had to have a confrontation with her. Since the mom was dealing with an Authority Figure, she didn't snap or guilt-trip like she would have with the bridesmaids she wasn't afraid of!" says Claire, a recent bridesmaid from Boston.

The Coordinator Cuts the Guest List

If you have a bride's mom who is pushing extra names onto the shower guest list, the coordinator can step in to remind her—with authority the mom respects more readily, but also with diplomacy and respect—that the bridesmaids are on a budget. The pro can thus save you a fortune.

Now, not all moms are pushy, bossy, or in need of a talking-to. Most are quite wonderful to work with, eager to participate with the maid of honor in the lead, and happy to hand over a check for whatever the group plans. They're honored to be invited to help plan, and most often, they're an asset to the group. And you may be able to plan a far, far better bridal shower with them involved than if they weren't. So cheers to those awesome moms who are great team players!

SIZE

The golden rule of bridal shower etiquette is that you never invite some-one to a shower who isn't invited to the wedding. Period. So if—as has happened quite often recently—the bride submits a guest wish list that includes people who aren't on her small wedding guest list, you have to dis-cuss with her that she's making a grave mistake. Guests will get offended if they're invited to and attend a shower, and then no wedding invitation ever arrives. That's a bridge-burner. Show her this paragraph if you have to. She has to go by etiquette rules, as does the maid of honor, the moms, and anyone else who adds names to the guest list.

These days, most hosts invite to the bridal shower only the absolute closest relatives and friends, not every single woman or couple invited to the wedding. In many families, there's a happy understanding that not everyone can be invited to the shower. And most people are just fine with it. In some large families, there's even an unwritten rule that some closer cousins are invited, while others are not. And some relatives and friends are relieved when they're *not* on the A-list. It gives them their Saturday back, and they don't have to get an extra gift. Tough economic times do veer some people to this mind-set.

So to keep your bridal shower costs under control, remind the group leaders that smaller shower guest lists mean a nicer party can be planned, the bride can mingle with all of her guests more easily, and no one is bur-dened with an enormous cost.

The Average Number of Guests

Different families have different circles of close relatives and friends, so some showers have 15 guests and some have (gulp!) 150.

The bride's guest list, which she often hands over even when the shower is going to be a surprise, is the guest list you'll work from, and it's okay to ask her or her mom to provide full names and mailing addresses for the most proper invitation-sending plan. And while the bride may go to her *wedding* guest list when regrets come in, *you do not have to do this*. Don't put yourself under any pressure to have a huge turnout as some sign that the bride is loved by a large number of people. A smaller, more intimate group can show plenty of love for the guest(s) of honor.

Now if the wedding will be a destination wedding, it *is* okay to give the couple a bridal shower beforehand. Yes, this is bending the etiquette rule saying all shower guests must be invited to the wedding, but it's a growing trend, provided guest lists are kept super-small.

And most shower hosts do not invite the bride's bosses and co-workers to the shower, so that may be a few more names to keep off the list.

STYLE

Setting the style for the bridal shower is the fun part. You have so many options open to you, and it's your planning choices *within the styles* that save your budget. There's no one style that automatically saves. So, you can have an elegantly catered luncheon at the country club for $60 per guest, and a gorgeous, tented, at-home bridal shower for the *same* $60 per guest if you've loaded the menu with lots of pricey dishes, and you're giving out favor swag bags filled with pricey take-home gifts.

With that in mind, that it's your choices within the party's style that determine your budget, you may find that a particular style of party *allows you more opportunities to save, while still impressing*.

So let's take them one at a time, and take notes on each to see which ones your group finds most suiting to the bride's style *and* to your budget as a whole:

BRIDESMAID ON A BUDGET

Formal Evening Dinner at a Restaurant or Country Club

• The restaurant or country club will most often present you with several different menus to choose from. Their basic menu may have three courses including gourmet fare, plus a cake and desserts, plus open bar.

• Their next-level-up menu may include a buffet of cold seafood options, a lavish salad bar, four courses, a dessert bar, and international coffees.

• And their platinum package might add carving and seafood stations, lobster tails, and any number of top-tier menu delights.

Formal Afternoon Buffet at a Restaurant or Country Club

• The menus may be the same as the formal evening party, just for 40 percent less, owing to the afternoon hours.

• An elegant afternoon buffet may include hot chafing dishes, a hummus station, a sushi station, and a number of desserts.

Formal Evening Buffet at Home, Catered

• You contact your choice of off-site caterer and choose from a number of menu packages, including hot chafing dishes, salads, hot passed hors d'oeuvres presented on silver platters by their wait staff, and a number of other elegant touches.

• You might hire the caterer to prepare and deliver the chafing dishes, salads, breads, and then you'll provide the cake and desserts from your own baker.

Formal Afternoon Buffet at Home, Catered

• The same goes, with the caterer providing your choices of menu items from different categories.

• Some catering companies will provide staff to work your buffet line, and hand-pass hors d'oeuvres in your home and out on your terrace.

Luncheon at a Restaurant

• It may be a sit-down luncheon from a prix-fixe menu, including three to four courses, and your guests' choices of desserts from three options.

• A new trend in luncheons is combination platters, with trios of desserts for half the price.

Luncheon at Home
• You might have it catered, or you might DIY your menu.
• Since you're your own caterer, the service is often up to you, including bar service.

Evening Cocktail Party
• At a restaurant or at home, the fare is elegant evening formal, most often an array of six to twelve hand-passed hors d'oeuvres, with a sizeable buffet of hot dishes and salads.
• The cocktail party may take place in your home, with you self-catering or DIYing your dishes, and setup and cleanup are your domain.

Brunch
• The brunch is one of the fastest-growing styles in popularity, with many hotels offering lavish buffets of hot and cold dishes, carving stations, omelette stations, seafood bars, and dessert bars—plus a free mimosa for each guest—at just under $25 per person on a non-holiday weekend.
• Brunch catered at your home may include hot chafing dishes, quiches, luncheon-type dishes, and desserts you can cater in or DIY.

Tea Party
• Old-world elegance comes to your celebration when you book a tea party at a hotel ballroom or estate home, with finger sandwiches and light salads on the menu, along with baked items such as scones, muffins, and cookies.
• A tea party may be hosted at your home, even with a pro caterer, but most often DIY-planned and self-catered with trays of sandwiches and baked items from Costco or your supermarket's catering department.

Backyard Barbecue

• This one trips up many party planners, since a barbecue menu might be upscale, including filet mignons and bacon-wrapped shrimp and scallops on skewers, strip steaks, chicken breasts, grilled vegetables, and plenty of salads ... not budget-friendly.

• An informal barbecue that suits the bride and groom's style may include burgers and hot dogs, with lots of fresh salads, pickles, deviled eggs, and fruit salad for dessert along with a sheet cake. This style is a favorite at $10 per guest, and then you can add in one or two menu indulgences like grilled shrimp kebobs and microbrew beers.

Formal Evening Dessert Party

• For a change of pace, you might plan an evening dessert party, at which guests feast on chocolate mousse served in martini glasses, tartlets, slices of red velvet cake, chocolate-dipped berries, and plenty of champagne.

I offer these descriptions just to get you envisioning the different types of party styles, and we'll get into far, far more detail about the most affordable and still remarkable menu items in Chapter 10.

At-home parties often require additional rentals of tables, china, and perhaps even tents and the hiring of bartenders and servers—all of which is often included at a restaurant or country club—so again, there's no way to say that an at-home barbecue is always going to be the least expensive style. The tea party may be a winner at $12 per guest, but ... and this is the *priceless* question: Is it the bride and groom's style of celebration?

When the group narrows down the possibilities of the shower's style, you can then move on to the next considerations to maximize your budget.

TIMING

Bridal showers usually take place between three and six weeks prior to the wedding, but this, too, is subject to the new flexibilities of etiquette: whatever works best for the bride. In the past, the bride and all of her bridesmaids, and probably most of the guests, lived within a close range of the wedding's location. Now, the bride might live clear across the country, or a few hours away. So, the shower will need to be planned for a weekend when she'll be in town. Thus, many bridal parties find themselves planning a bridal shower three months before the wedding, during the bride's visit to her hometown for the holidays.

And there's the challenge. If the bride is only in town during Thanksgiving weekend or Memorial Day weekend, your bridal shower plans might be subject to sites' and vendors' higher prices on those in-demand weekends. Your costs could go up 30 percent or more when you need to book a site during a peak time. That hotel's brunch might be $50 per person on Thanksgiving weekend, rather than its usual $20 per person on a non-holiday weekend. It's something to think about.

Look at your calendar, and see where your most affordable bridal shower date falls as related to the wedding. If the wedding will be in April, then you could plan the shower for the far less expensive catering month of March, or even ultra-affordable February—just not Valentine's Day weekend. An October wedding could put your party plans smack in the middle of ultra-pricy August. Fall weddings present big challenges for bridal shower planners, since peak events season is in full swing for months prior. So you may have to book during peak time, and find other ways to save if the calendar doesn't help you out.

Ask your site or caterer to show you their package sheets for different date ranges, *since each site or vendor claims different dates for their peak and off-peak seasons.* A restaurant might begin their top-priced plans on May 1, while another might bring out those higher-priced menus on May 31. By shifting your shower date to the first weekend in May, even though it's eight weeks before the wedding, you could save hundreds of dollars . . . and the bride may be ultra-surprised to walk into her party then.

"With so many of us living in different states and the bride herself far away and his family living overseas, we threw the bridal shower three days before the wedding when everyone would be in town for the big day," says one brilliant bridesmaid from Minneapolis. "We had to tell the bride about it, since those days would be hectic for her, and she just blocked off those few hours that day to relax and enjoy herself, so it worked out perfectly . . . and we just got into off-peak November catering dates! We saved $500!"

LOCATION

Obviously, the fanciest country club in town is going to have elevated prices, and even their basic package might cost triple what you'll find at a wonderful restaurant's private party room. So while you and the rest of the bridesmaids embark upon a menu-gathering research campaign, keep in mind some important budget rules when it comes to different *types* of locations.

• Non-bridal sites often charge less for their catering packages than traditional bridal sites like hotel ballrooms and banquet halls. So a restaurant's catering packages may range from 20 to 40 percent less for a comparable menu.

• Look into unique sites such as museums, art galleries, botanical gardens, and estate homes—all of which invite private parties as an extra revenue stream. These sites *may* have their own list of approved caterers that you can hire, and some state that you must use their one, chosen catering company that's familiar to them, insured, licensed, and not likely to burn down their building. Many sites allow you to bring in your own caterers, as well. Keep in mind that these sites charge a fee to use their establishment and grounds, so do the math and see if the savings are still there.

• Look into your alumni connections. A few years out of college, and we all forget that we are lifetime beneficiaries of the perks. Many alma maters will grant you big discounts on uses of *their* surprisingly attractive party spaces—which they use for their centennial balls, sports team victory parties, fund-raising dinners, and other elaborate events—as well as the private gardens often used by the dean and faculty members for their teas and other events. For half the price of a ballroom party, you could land a fabulous setting that honors the bride and groom's cherished alma mater.

• Check out nearby bed-and-breakfast establishments, which often don't charge a site fee and allow you to use their gardens and grounds for your party.

• Botanical gardens and parks welcome private parties, and many have private ballrooms featuring lofty ceilings, marble fireplaces, terraces overlooking *amazing* gardens . . . or you might be able to book their outdoor party site with a gazebo. These sites, too, may prescribe a list of approved or in-house caterers, and if these pros can help you create a fantastic budget menu, you may have just found the prettiest home for your party. A site fee is likely to be charged, and be aware that some of the larger, better-known botanical gardens' site fees are astronomical, so check out the tourism department website in your area to find *additional* gardens and park areas you can select.

• Ocean- or lake-view restaurants offer atmosphere and a great view, as well as a match to your beach theme, but many do hike up their prices because they *know* they're in demand. Not all, but many. Comparison-shop carefully with these sites.

• Church halls have in greater number remodeled their celebration rooms, with some featuring fabulous parquet dance floors and window treatments. If they require the use of their parishioner cooking teams, this could be a price-friendly choice that allows the bride to celebrate in a location that's meaningful to her.

Use Where You Fit In

"The groom is a firefighter, so we asked the fire chief if we could get permission to use the firehouse's private party room for the couple's coed shower. It was a great, blank space with lots of round tables and chairs we wouldn't have to rent, and once we decorated it and self-catered, our total was $750 less than if we held the shower at a restaurant. And we could use the site for more than the four hours a restaurant would allow us."

—CINDY, A MAID OF HONOR IN NEW JERSEY

• Does a parent have a membership at a private association? Maybe that Junior League's well-appointed party room or the Elk Club's lodge with its wood-beamed ceilings and fireplaces and mahogany bar would be fantastic, especially with the member discount given to your planning-partner parent.

• Libraries now welcome private parties in their event rooms, and they, too, may have been remodeled lately with enormous windows and sky-lights, carpeting, and tables and chairs to use for the party. And the bride won't suspect that she's walking into her shower when you ask her to come with you to drop off your overdue library books.

• Cultural associations are *everywhere*, with their lavish party rooms and their member chefs preparing authentic meals honoring the bride and/or groom's heritage. These organizations are the big, hot trend right now for themed parties, and their prices are often one-third the cost of hotel or restaurant packages, even with a site fee charged.

• Additional unique sites include wineries, theaters' event rooms, aquariums, zoo party rooms, and friends' beach or ski homes they let you use as their gift to the bride.

Better to Buy?

Consider this: It can cost $1 to $2 per wineglass for a rental. And it can cost *less* than $1 per wineglass to buy them from Ikea, Target, Crate & Barrel, or Bed Bath & Beyond. So as a group, you can buy a few boxes of twenty glasses each, keep the sectioned boxes for future storage, and for *the same price* as what you'd spend on rentals, you all have stylish glasses to take home for your future cocktail parties and family celebrations.

And then we have the at-home party mentioned earlier in this chapter. It may seem like hosting the bridal shower at home is a guaranteed money-saver, but that is only true *if* you have enough seating, china, wineglasses, utensils, table linens, and serving platters to suit your party. If not, you're going to have the added expenses of rentals. And that can add up. Here's how to beat the rentals budget crunch, to make that at-home party the perfect place for your affordable shower:

• First, see what you can borrow from your co-hosts and also from guests. Grandma might be able to bring over a dozen of her silver serving platters that she uses every Thanksgiving. Aunt Beth can bring over her punch bowl. Friends can bring over their warming plates and electric chafing dishes. Work your network to see what can be removed from your rentals shopping list, saving hundreds.

• Talk to your caterer to see if he or she provides serving platters along with the food. You might not need to worry about getting extra ones.

• Ask friends to recommend a great rentals agency that delivers and picks up, and allows you to pack plates, silverware, and glasses back in their delivery crates *unwashed*. That's way better than needing to run the dishwasher ten times during and after the party! Friends who have hosted weddings and big family parties have already done comparison-shopping, so ask whom they found to be the best-priced. And of course, your party coordinator has a list of the best-priced shops in town.

• Here is a guiding list for how much you'll need to rent so that you have enough of each essential item, yet not too big of an order:

> • Plan to get enough wine and cocktail glasses for each guest to have two drinks the first hour of the party, then one drink for each hour after that.
>
> • For small appetizer or cocktail party buffet plates, rent 5 small plates per person.
>
> • For larger dinner plates, the general rule in rental world is 1.5 plates per person, allowing half of your guests to fill plates a second time. If you know you have big eaters on your guest list, go for two plates per person.
>
> • Another rule out there is to rent 10 percent more plates than your guest head count.
>
> • Don't forget to rent an entire extra set of plates for cake and desserts. Again, 1.5 plates per person suffices.
>
> • Rent one set of utensils per guest, and add an extra 10 percent more to your order.
>
> • If you'll rent table linens, be extra careful about taking the actual measurements of your tables so that all of your linens hang appropriately and attractively on your guest

tables. (You may be able to use your own or a relative's or friend's pretty tablecloth for the cake table.)

- A five-foot round table will seat ten guests comfortably. Rent the better models of tables and chairs to avoid rickety, collapsing, ugly ones.

Additional Items to Borrow, Not Rent

- Coolers
- Grills
- Strings of lights
- Coffeemaker
- Espresso maker
- Cappuccino maker
- Fondue pots
- Chocolate fountain
- Pitchers
- Trays
- Dessert pedestals
- Cake plates
- Serving utensils

- Candleholders
- Candelabras
- Ice buckets
- Blenders
- Fans, for hot days
- Space heaters, for cool days or evenings
- Specialty party machines, like a bubble machine a friend may have
- Seasonal décor items
- Kids' games, if children are on the guest list

So with borrowing and buying under your belt, it's time to talk about tents. Some sites won't allow you to put up a tent on their grounds, since the stakes and poles damage their lawns. So ask before you put down a deposit on a tent. If you'll put up a tent in your backyard, be sure to rent the highest-quality structure you can afford. Now is not the time to scrimp, since cheaper models tend to sag and not handle wind and rain well. And some are just ugly. This is one investment it's smarter to budget more for, as well as for quality flooring tiles that snap together, providing for attractive and safe floor surfaces for your guests to walk and dance on. Your rental agent can help you figure out how much tent and flooring space you'll need, as well as how to maximize the shape of your yard, maybe even using special tent attachments to wrap the tent around your existing trees and alongside your house for extra party room.

Work your network to see who can bring what, making your at-home or nontraditional location more affordable. Even Martha Stewart shows mismatched china patterns and teacups in her magazine, adding extra visual appeal and creativity, so there's no pressure to make sure each china set a friend can bring will match perfectly. Send out a call for borrowed items, and then you'll return the favor with your case of wineglasses the next time someone else is hosting a party.

INVITATIONS

With your modest guest list agreed upon, your site chosen, and other details set, it's time to *invite* the guests to the party. *Free* invitations sites lead the budget-saving trend, especially since sites like Evite.com now have gorgeous, designer styled shower invitations that you can send to guests and enjoy the organization factor of their online responses.

If you'd rather use the traditional, printed invitations, here are some ways to save:

• Skip the pricey boxed invitation kits at the craft store, which can be marked up 20 percent or more than the prices of buying papers and envelopes individually.

• Visit the same budget invitation websites the bride is going to, such as Invitations4sale.com for 40 percent off expertly printed invitations.

• Stick with single-panel invitations rather than foldout or tri-fold cards.

• Stick with one color and style of font, to avoid extra charges that some companies apply for using two or more styles.

• Eliminate vellums and foil layers, which are not needed for today's print methods, but are just ornamental.

• Go with smaller invitations that cost less to order and mail.

• Stick with regular, rectangular invitations, since squares often cost extra to mail due to their unique shape.

• Use regular envelopes, and avoid the extra expense of shiny envelope liners.

• Skip the pearlized borders and other special effects that raise the prices.

• If you know of a recent bride who bought invitation-making software—I love the under-$25 software from Mountaincow.com!—ask if you can stop by to design your invites using her program.

• Design your DIY invites without big, color graphics that take up a lot of extra ink, and use simple, elegant line accents instead to eliminate the need for an extra $35 ink cartridge.

• Find fabulous invitation papers and card stock at the office supply store or craft store, using a coupon or online coupon code to save 15 percent or more off your supply budget.

• Shop for pretty invitation cards and envelopes at Mountaincow.com, one of my favorite sources for discount bridal print items.

• Skip the glitter, ribbon-bow, glue-on charms, and other accents, and just design a pretty print style that needs no extra décor.

• Skip extra inserts, such as a response postcard. It's okay to put RSVP information right on the invitation.

• If you'll include inserts, such as a recipe card for guests to fill out, take one completed, stuffed invitation to the post office to be weighed to make sure standard postage rates will cover you. It's a huge mistake to send out too-heavy invites, have them all come back to you, and then to have to start over with new envelopes and double the postage expense.

• And of course, making the invitations could be a parent's contribution to the shower expenses, making it free for you! The maid of honor can share this concept with moms, grandmoms, and others who volunteer to help out in any way needed. Resourceful bridal parties do "farm out" some tasks when requested, which allows their budget to breathe and the volunteer to contribute this $30 or so task *as their bridal shower gift, saving them $50 or more in present money.* It's a win-win, if you have a pool of DIY artists, or if one of the money-challenged bridesmaids wants to take on this task as her share of the bridal party plans.

CHAPTER 9

Planning the Bridal Shower—Décor

*Y*our pretty party requires a pretty scene, and you don't have to spend a fortune to achieve impressive décor. In this section, you'll create your plan for designing décor on the cheap . . . without it looking cheap. Say good-bye to those balloons and those yards and yards of spiral-twisted streamers. Not only are they very 1980s, they're just not cost-effective. And yes, they do look to some like the work of a cheapo bridal party. Here's how to make your party space stand out:

SETTING THE TABLE

Bring a little bit of color to your guest tables by setting them with colored tablecloths and napkins. You could rent them, or you could ask around your circle of bridesmaids to see who has or can borrow pink tablecloths. They don't have to match. A mauve tablecloth can be used for the main table or cake table. One long, light pink tablecloth can set the buffet table. Your circle of co-planners can achieve this décor foundation without spending a dime.

Or, if white tablecloths are easier to acquire, add some accent with colored table runners, which you can make with $10 worth of fabric and the hemming skills of a DIY volunteer.

Plastic party table coverings from the party supply store may be inexpensive, but they *look* inexpensive, so it's always best to see what you can achieve before turning to that option as a last resort.

For your table settings, ideally you'll be using regular plates, not paper ones that are harsh on the environment and again evoke the cheapo approach. You may be able to choose colored plates from the restaurant's supply if that's where you're hosting the shower, or you may be able to rent thirty or forty pretty pastel plates—an expense made do-able by all of your other cost-cuts in your shower plans.

An easy way to add color to your table setting is to get napkin rings—for under $1 at the craft store for the most basic designs—and accent each with a single, small flower or a tiny tuft of teeny flowers. For just $10 to $15 total, you can get the flowers from your grocery store inexpensively and DIY over forty napkin rings. Just this small pop of color, done so affordably, makes a standard-set table come alive.

CENTERPIECES

Leave the big floral arrangements to the bride's budget as her wedding reception centerpiece of choice, and use flowers in a more budget-friendly way:

• Set one single, wide flower such as a peony, hydrangea section, a single gardenia, or a rose in a low-set bowl or small square vase that you pick up at the craft store for just a few dollars apiece, less if you buy by the case.

• Use your own and borrowed vases for each table to hold a bunch of low-priced flowers such as stock, filler, daisies, in-season tulips, or other non-pricey blooms. Wander through the floral department at your grocery store and check out the flowers that *aren't roses*, those clusters of tiny white flowers or tiny yellow flowers meant to be sold as additions to larger, rose-filled centerpieces. *Those*, at $4.99 per bunch, can be your centerpiece blooms, filling six to eight vases per bunch.

• Set three or four small votive candles in holders in a diamond shape at the center of the table as the only centerpiece you'll need, at a great savings over floral centerpieces, and get that floral look by scattering rose petals on the tablecloth around them. Since a single rose yields dozens of usable petals when carefully pulled apart, you'll likely only need a dozen roses in one $14.99 bunch to grace all of your tables.

• Ask the site—if you'll be at a hotel or restaurant—*if they provide the centerpieces*. Some sites provide floral bunch centerpieces as their usual method of setting each table, so you might find that you don't have to spend a thing. They're already taking care of it for you!

• If a mom or grandmom is looking for a way to contribute to the costs of the shower, paying for the centerpieces is one of the most popular choices for them to take on. Talk with the maid of honor to see if the moms or grandmoms would like to pitch in.

• Decorate with rose petals scattered on the table around a single pillar candle.

• Center your tables with bread baskets assembled from the bread collection off the buffet line.

• Fill vases with colorful, color-coordinated candies.

• Fill vases with single- or multihued flower petals.

• Center each table with framed photos of the wedding couple.

DANGLING DÉCOR

You see these tissue paper bells and balls in the party supply store. You just pull open the accordion-style décor, clip it into shape, and *voila!* You have a nice, 1960s-era décor ball to hang from the ceiling. Unless you're planning a retro party, skip these cliché décor balls. Even priced under $8 or so each, they still take a chunk out of the budget.

A big trend in budget party décor is copying celebrity event designer style and making it "rain" flowers or crystals. Here's how it works: Individual flowers are wired to—or multi-lengths of clear or colored crystals are tied to—a length of clear, plastic fishing-type line. You can make it easy and just attach the flower or crystal at the end of the wire, or you can affix flowers or crystals every six inches or so along the line for a multi-tiered effect.

Each decorated line costs $1 or so with all supplies from the craft store, and you can hang them in a cluster, such as over the bride's table (as if she were being rained on, a.k.a. showers of happiness), over the cake table, in a corner of the room, over displayed photos of the bride and groom, or however you'd like, to whichever degree you'd like. Stick with simpler crystals or smaller flowers to keep your costs down, since you could certainly twist a budget idea into a budget-*buster* by selecting the expensive, fancy crystals or pricey gardenias for the raining effect.

FOOD AND CAKE TABLE DÉCOR

If you have extra votive holders and flower petals, you can certainly place or sprinkle them on the cake table around the cake to get double-duty from your décor supply. But there's *no need* to buy extra décor to surround the cake, like you see done at weddings. A simple, elegant cake, or a theme cake, garners all the attention and doesn't need additional décor for a shower.

Watch Out!

If the wedding itself will be a small one on a modest budget, you never want to outdo what the bride has planned for her big day. So scale down your décor plans so that you don't steal her spotlight.

To dress up your buffet table and stations, here are some budget-friendly ideas:

• Instead of a big floral arrangement in a vase for over $50, fill that vase with stand-up veggies such as celery arranged to look like a floral décor, and accent with big sprigs of parsley or rosemary tucked into the arrangement. You use the leftovers from your DIY meal preps as table décor, and you spend *nothing* extra to dress up your tables.

• Instead of having a basket of rolls at the end of the buffet table or set on each guest table, decorate your food tables with small platters piled with unique breads such as foccaccia, grissini, wheat rolls, onion rolls, and other baked goodies that now add visual appeal to your tables *for not a dime extra*. Just ask the restaurant.

• Votive candles and pillar candles need to stay off the food tables, since a guest can get singed or even caught on fire when they're reaching for a canapé and their sleeve goes over a flickering candle. Save tons of money by skipping the décor pillar candles and tapers when it comes to your food tables. Instead, use those extra votive candle holders you have on hand, and fill them with sand and shells if you're having a beach theme.

• Look at how the top restaurants and resorts dress up their food stations, noticing that they sometimes use oversized platters and fill just the center of that enormous pasta bowl with their gourmet menu item. When big, beautiful platters fill the table, there's no need to provide extra décor. Be sure your platters match or coordinate, and that all serving spoons and ladles come from the same or coordinating collection for a unified look that gives the impression of costing lots of money . . . even though you own or borrowed every piece. Again, it might be worth the investment for you to buy a $9.99 set of three white party platters from the B Smith collection at Bed Bath & Beyond, use it for this party at a big savings over rentals, and then keep them for future parties and holiday dinners.

LIGHT UP THE ROOM

Creating great lighting effects is a top way that celebrity party planners turn their décor plans into extraordinary visions, and you can do the same without hiring Hollywood lighting teams that work on movies or light up buildings for the Oscars.

Ask your site manager if you can arrange for any special lighting effects, such as having a spotlight trained on the cake—as seen at many a celebrity wedding—or using pin lights over each of the tables. Many restaurants and hotel ballrooms can easily rearrange their pin and track lighting to achieve your wished-for effect, and many won't charge you for this simple task that their events crew can create.

Since most bridal showers take place in the daytime, natural light is going to brighten the room if you'll be in a place with big windows or an outdoor terrace. At a home-based bridal shower, the same benefits of free lighting courtesy of Mother Nature apply, so you won't need to take extra steps for lighting, or set out candles for décor.

If your shower will take place in the evening, though—as many coed bridal showers do—investing some time and perhaps a little bit of money for lighting accents is well worth it. But the biggest challenge in lighting is often the price of candles. The really pretty ones at home décor stores can cost over $30. Apiece. So here's your cheat sheet to get a fabulous supply of candles without spending that much to decorate your entire party space:

- Buy cases of unscented votive candles low-priced at craft shops.

- Stores like Target and Walmart stock cases of votive and small pillar candles in their party supply sections.

- Check your local warehouse store like Costco, Sam's Club, and BJ's to find candle cases ... and you may save 30 percent or more than craft store prices.

- Check the candle section at Bed Bath & Beyond, Ikea, and other home décor stores to see if they've stocked cases of candles at $1 apiece. Stay away from name-brand, scented candles and just look for standard, no-name collections in boxes or even in bags on the cheap.

- I've seen bags of votive candles, thirty-six for $4 at Forever 21 in the candles and décor section, so be willing to explore the other departments of stores where you normally shop for clothing and accessories!

- Hit post-holiday candle sales at the craft store and at card shops for 50 percent or more off white or colored votives and votive holders. After Easter, shops want to unload those pastel candles on the cheap.

- Look in the wedding crafts sections of craft stores to find cases of bridal white or pastel votive candles, set there for DIY projects such as pinning florals onto the sides, priced lower than their home décor candles.

- Order online only if there's no shipping charge involved.

• Check eBay for fantastic prices and auctions on cases of candles. Craft stores and artisans often list their overstock there to recycle and also make a bit of money back on their investment. I just found a set of twenty-four simple, white votives about to sell at auction for 99 cents. And I also saw lots of 144 pink votive candles *and* classic glass holders up for grabs at $50.00, which is enough to decorate your party space beautifully. If your four co-bridesmaids split the cost with you, it's $10 for your share of a celeb-worthy sea of mood-setting candles.

• Decorate your own candles, votive or pillar, with simple stick-in crystal-headed or pearl-headed pins at the craft store for $4 per bags of twenty-four pins.

• To make your décor candles last longer, pop them in the freezer over-night, which slows their burning speed and allows them to last all the way through your party.

Freebie Candles

If you'll be at a restaurant or hotel party room, ask your site manager if they have candles you can use for your décor. Many locations have a supply of candles that are either brand-new or leftovers from other events at which the candles burned for only a few hours. Ask if you can acquire those candles and holders and set them aflame for your party, which the site might provide for free, or charge you a stunningly low price to buy and get them out of their storeroom. Always ask what the site has that you can use!

CHAPTER 10

Planning the Bridal Shower— Food, Drinks, and Cake

*T*he food makes the party, and the cake sends guests home with a big smile on their faces. But as you know, party menus can be ultra-pricey with over 60 percent of any celebration's budget going to the appetizers, entrées, drinks, and desserts. If you're doing the math right now, you might be a bit worried about what you could possibly serve on *that* amount, but don't panic. There are plenty of ways to arrange a spectacular bridal shower menu on a budget. We'll take each category one at a time, serving up savings you'll love.

Brunch Is Best?

As a reminder from earlier in this book, a brunch might be the way to go, with your guests enjoying a hotel or restaurant's lavish weekend spread of breakfast and luncheon foods, a free mimosa, and a dessert buffet for under $15 or so per person. It's definitely worth looking into!

One of the first suggestions that may come up is getting party platters from a supermarket—those big trays of dozens of wraps and finger sandwiches, buffalo wings, tomato and mozzarella slices, and other goodies. While you may be able to find a great price at discount sites like Costco's catering department, keep in mind that supermarket and caterer platters often cost 30 percent more than trays you could assemble yourself. I looked at some platters at my nearby supermarket and saw a fruit patter for over $50! No joke! A cheese platter was $34. If I bought bunches of fruit and assembled my own platter, it would have cost under $20. So think twice about convenience platters, and recruit your fellow bridesmaids to shop for the ingredients, chop veggies, and cube fruit to make your own food platters for less.

Speaking of DIY menu items, some guests love to contribute their own dishes to the party. If you hear from volunteers, take them up on it! And tell them their dip platter or sandwich tray is their gift for the bride. They'll love saving over 60 percent on what they would have spent on a gift from the registry. Talk to the maid of honor first before you offer this deal to kindhearted volunteers, though. The chief of party planning might not want to tread that etiquette.

THE MENU

Here you'll find out the best budget-saving secrets for courses and dishes that you can include in *any* style of shower—from cocktail party to luncheon to desserts-only party. Pick out the ones that apply to your group's plans and rack up those savings in tasty ways!

Snacks

• One of the biggest party budget-wasters is overbuying on the snacks, nuts, and other munchies. Party hosts set out big bowls of chips or pretzels, snack mix, and nuts, and hours later, hardly anything has been touched, and you have to throw everything out. Instead, just pour no more than a cup of snacks in each bowl, wait to see if they're so good your guests finish them off, and refresh the supply once or twice during the party.

• The same goes for dips. Just a small amount set out, the rest goes in the fridge for later, and you can refresh if you need more guacamole or hummus in any bowl. The savings equal a killer 80 percent when you're not throwing out most of what you bought.

• Just two different chips styles is enough for any party.

• In the supermarket, look *down* at the brands and bags stocked on the bottom shelves where the savings are. Those tempting, creative-flavor, overpriced snack bags are intentionally positioned at eye level so that you'll buy them. But the savings packs are down low on the shelves, or up on the top shelf. Shop from there.

• Make your own party mix, using bulk mini-pretzels, corn chips, wasabi peas, and other snacks, and following a spice and baking recipe at FoodTV .com to make triple the amount of snack mix—and get bragging rights!—than if you bought a $6 bag from the store.

Appetizers

• Have pricier shrimp cocktail and clams hand-passed by servers— either you, teen relatives who want to "work" your event for a small amount of pay, or wait staff that your group hires to work your event. With these expensive apps passed instead of displayed on a buffet table, guests eat 40 percent less!

• DIY "pinwheels" of rolled tortillas filled with a cheesy vegetable spread, like Alouette, and cut into bites costs far less than buying pinwheel platters from a caterer.

• Skip the big cheese platter, which can be very pricey—I've seen them for over $50!—and instead offer a cheese course of 3 to 4 different types of cheese cut into cubes or slices and served with a slice of melon or grapes.

• Pita triangles and hummus are always popular as appetizer choices, so either DIY your favorite hummus or pick up ready-made containers of Sabra brand or organic hummus as your indulgence buy. *Not every food has*

to be low-budget! Including two or three splurges makes your entire menu look more exorbitant! Check out the red pepper hummus and other flavors, or go to FoodTV.com to find hummus recipes you can make as a solo or group effort.

• Dips are one of the popular dishes at parties, but they also go to waste, so make a *small* bowl of spinach dip or onion dip—DIY costs less!—and just get 1 to 2 bags of whole grain dipping chips to go with them.

• Don't go crazy with the chips! This is one of the biggest budget-busters, with party hosts overbuying multiple bags. Just two bags of chips is fine for a 30-person party.

• A single pizza—veggie-topped to please your vegetarian guests, Sicilian, or "grandma's pizza"-style—can be cut into squares as a great appetizer for under $10.

• Break out your slow cooker to whip up crowd-pleasing Swedish or barbecue meatballs. Again, make your own—skipping those pricey premade turkey meatballs in the grocery store meat cooler—and feed a dozen guests for under $5.

• For boxes of frozen appetizers, such as those puff pastries filled with cheese and spinach or little wrapped hot dogs, go for the budget, bulk boxes at discount warehouse stores like Costco if the *price per unit* mark shows a lower figure. The twelve-piece boxes of frozen apps can often cost *twice* the per-unit expense!

• Go fresh and in-season, choosing from caterer's lists of what's available now. Veggies and fruits that are in-season cost far less than those that have to be imported.

• Shop at the best-priced supermarkets in town, even if you regularly shop at pricier grocery stores. You'll find the veggies are just as fresh and shiny, but may cost 20 percent less.

• If you have a favorite gourmet market or eatery, here's a fun secret: Many of them are not open on Sundays, so they put their stock of fresh dishes, soups, salads, sandwiches, and entrées on sale for 50 percent off starting at 2 p.m. or so on Saturday. If your shower takes place on Sunday, you may be able to load up on gorgeous, gourmet salads and foods for *half*

the price! Ask around at those gourmet eateries to see what their weekend sales are like, and if they don't have a bargain sale each weekend, *ask if you can be granted a big discount for coming in and scooping up their Saturday stock.* Asking can get you a fabulous deal and amazing foods for the shower.

• For spring rolls, sushi, and other handmade, fresh appetizers, those little eight-packs you see in the grocery store display cases can cost $6 to $8 each! That's $1 per bite! Instead, visit a Japanese or Vietnamese restaurant and ask if they provide party platters for budget parties. I've found amazing prices this way, and fabulously authentic dishes.

• If you'll serve a salad, make it unique and special by giving guests the chance to add their own garbanzo beans, cauliflower bites, and goat cheese sprinklings, all available at the supermarket as "sides" that make a budget-friendly salad stand out. And DIY your dressing to avoid paying $5 a pop for salad dressing bottles.

A Money-Saving Don't!

For an at-home party, don't try to save money by putting out your own, half used bottles of dressing. Guests worry about contamination, you look cheap, and all of your great work on the shower gets tarnished by this obviously cheapo step!

• Contact your local family farms to see if you can buy a bushel of produce from them at a budget price. Many farms harvest way too much, and they welcome these custom calls from party planners so that they can make some money on what would otherwise go to waste. Call them directly, though, rather than shopping at farmer's markets where some farm sales teams overcharge for tomatoes, fruits, lettuces, and the like.

• How's *your* garden? You might have enough tomato and basil plants out back to make a phenomenal, fresh batch of bruschetta (tomato salad)

or salsa for *nothing!* My bruschetta recipe: Dice 6 tomatoes, 1 shallot, and 2 minced garlic heads, and mix together with 3 to 4 tablespoons of *fresh*, chopped basil. Add 3 tablespoons of red wine vinegar and 1 tablespoon of 100 percent virgin olive oil, mix together, and serve on top of baguette slices that have been brushed with a small amount of olive oil, briefly toasted to barely-there brownness.

• Ask your fellow bridesmaids and party hosts if their gardens can yield some party dishes, too.

Stations

• If the party will be at a restaurant or hotel, arrange to have just three or four stations, as the budget package may allow, rather than thinking you have to impress guests with five or six stations. Again, let the wedding shine in that regard.

• Skip the carved meat station.

• Skip the raw seafood station, and just use seafood as a garnish on an entrée or a topper for soup shots at a fall or winter party.

• Asian noodle stations are all the rage, with gourmet soba noodles served with fresh, steamed veggies made-to-order by the attendant. Celebrity caterers say this is one of the most deceptively inexpensive station options, and even the stars ask for noodle stations at their parties.

• Veggie stations are often on the budget package list, with Mediterranean veggie stations all the rage. Talk to the caterer to see how the Budget List stations can be chosen to complement each other.

• A pasta station is always a big hit with guests *when you offer a unique spin on pasta*. Since guests may not often get pumpkin-filled ravioli or mushroom sauce-topped rotini, it seems to them like you spent more. Sauces always make inexpensive pasta dishes look and taste more gourmet.

> ### *Sauce Is the Answer!*
>
> Dress up your pasta and inexpensive chicken dishes with a great, creative sauce, and it will always seem like you spent more than you did for this little catering trick!

Meats

• Yes, chicken and pork are the usual budget meat choices, and they can make your party when you select a more gourmet recipe, a sensational or spicy sauce, or even a kebob presentation, pairing marinated chicken cubes with veggies.

• Talk to your caterer about which meats will be in season at the time of your party. It might be surprising to know that some meats are in-season at certain times of year, which makes them better priced. And the current market rates also play a big part in your menu expense, so let your caterer tell you what's best-priced on the market right now.

• Keep meats to a minimum so that your healthy-eating, vegetarian, or vegan guests can partake in more of your dishes. It's a big mistake to load up on mostly meat dishes and see lots of it go to waste at the end of the party, when still-hungry guests leave unsatisfied because there was so little they could eat.

• Talk to your supermarket's butcher to see when they get their meat shipments, and when they mark down each packet of chicken, beef cubes, and other cuts. You may be able to arrange with the butcher to get a discount rate on mega-packs of meat.

Seafood

• You don't need to go wild with the seafood offerings as entrées or provide the raw seafood bar that may be part of the reception's fare. Just a touch as garnish or as a filling for ravioli goes a long way for less.

• Talk with your caterer or with the seafood specialist at your grocery store to see which seafoods are priced best on the market during the week of the party, so that you can get a selection of seafoods for way less than if you just stuck to a shopping list that includes salmon or other fish that might be more expensive due to weather or fishing issues. Be flexible, and you'll win.

• Check out the seafood offerings at discount warehouse stores like Costco, where you may be able to get fresh shrimp or frozen crab claws for half price.

• Be careful with bags of frozen shrimp from your grocer's freezer. Not only are they pricey for the three dozen or so pieces you'll get, the defrosting process might turn out slightly soggy shrimp cocktail.

• Stretch a smaller amount of seafood, such as including shrimp on barbecue or teriyaki skewers, interspersed with veggies.

• Include three grilled shrimp on an entrée combination platter alongside a few pieces of beef medallions or skillet-cooked chicken, plus a pretty side dish to save 40 percent on your entrées.

Mix It Up

On-site caterers say that when you give guests the chance to pick from three entrées, they have to buy enough of each type to allow your guests to change their minds! So they could be buying—and charging you for—triple the food! A combo-platter eliminates the extra expense, and guests get a delicious dish.

Pasta with Panache

• As an entrée or as a side, go unique with your pasta picks, choosing mushroom-stuffed ravioli or spinach and cheese tortellini—flavors your guests don't get every day, perhaps because their kids or spouses only like the basic stuff.

• Again, sauce up your pasta with a unique flavor, perhaps even a creamy crab sauce to get your seafood feature in there!

• At a family-style dinner, big bowls of baked ziti or cavatelli with broccoli are often crowd-pleasers and are among the least expensive dishes out there.

• Choose a unique shape of pasta, such as bow ties, to make a pasta dish seem more exciting, and your budget stays low.

Side Dishes

• If you're ordering platters from a caterer, look over the package form carefully, since some establishments *include* bread for free.

• A bulk pack of Pillsbury dinner rolls from Costco can be very cost-efficient, and if you pop them in the oven right before the party, your house will smell amazing!

• Make your own garlic bread by going to a bakery right before closing and buying end-of-day loaves of bread for half price, store them in sealed plastic bags, and then on party day, slice them, slather with olive oil or spread, sprinkle with garlic powder, and bake to yield a great amount of fresh, delicious garlic bread slices for the party.

• Some frozen bags of veggies can yield mushy, soggy results if you're not super-careful, so borrow a friend's steamer to DIY a side of steamed carrots, broccoli, or other crowd-pleasing sides.

• If you'll save by DIYing your own entrées and salads, consider getting your gourmet veggie sides catered. For my own rehearsal dinner, we catered in delicious, gorgeous sides like creamed spinach and five-cheese mac-and-cheese for under $40. *Again, some splurges make the rest of your menu stand out!*

• Can a mom or grandmom contribute to the party by making a few side dishes as her gift? Including family favorite recipes in the party makes it more special for the bride.

How Much Food Do You Need?

I spoke with several caterers to find out the Magic Formula of how much food is *really* needed to feed your guests. Here are the average amounts they suggested to keep you from over-buying—and overspending—yet to still have enough to please the crowd:

- Appetizers before a meal: 2 to 3 items per person, per hour

- Appetizers only, for a cocktail party: 5 to 6 items per person, per hour, which usually adds up to 12 to 15 items per person

- Chilled Salads: 4 ounces per person

- Hot Side Dishes: 3 to 4 ounces per person (depending on number of side dishes—with more than three side dishes, you can get away with 2 to 3 ounces per person)

- Pasta as an entrée: 6 to 8 ounces per person

- Pasta as a side dish: 3 to 4 ounces per person

- Lunch Entrée: 4 to 6 ounces per person for the entrée, plus 2 to 3 side dishes, bread, and salad

- Lunch Buffet: 4 ounces of meat or veggies per person, enough for everyone to have two sandwiches apiece

- Dinner Entrée: 6 to 8 ounces per person, plus 2 to 3 side dishes, bread, and salad

- Dessert: 3 to 4 ounces per person, or 1 slice of cake per person, or 4 to 5 ounces of creamy desserts like mousses or ice cream

- Rolls/Bread: 2 per person

- Fruit Platter: 3 to 5 pieces of sliced fruit per person

DRINKS

An open bar is a must at any party, since it's considered tacky to ask guests to travel to your fête, bring a gift, and then pay for their own drinks. To save on your drink menu, limit the choices of drink types—such as providing only three or four mixed drinks instead of an endless variety, eliminate shots and pricey lots-of-liquor drinks like Long Island iced teas from your menu, and offer your guests unique presentations of drinks as you'll see in the tips below.

Wines

• Do a little bit of research on WineSpectator.com and on FoodandWine.com to get the names and vintages of terrific, award-winning bottles of wine priced under $15 apiece—there are some great ones out there!

• Talk to the sales manager at your local discount liquor store to arrange a discount on your purchase of a case or two of wine.

• Stretch out your wine supply—and get twice as much for your money—by serving wine spritzers to your guests.

• Again, ask your fellow bridesmaids to bring along a bottle of wine or two from their own collections.

> ### *Always Have Enough*
>
> When a bar runs out of liquor or mixers, it's an obvious and embarrassing sign that you and the other hosts cut corners. So agree to shop generously, getting a few extra bottles of wine, a few extra twelve-packs of soda, and a few extra bottles of champagne and orange juice for mimosas . . . and you'll all divide and take the leftovers home.

Liquors

• Just serve two or three different signature cocktails, rather than supplying a full open bar of many different types of liquors and mixers.

• If you'd like to have a full open bar with tons of different liquors and more than three cocktail options, just have that open bar for three hours, instead of four, and close it down when it's time for coffee.

• Ask the other bridesmaids, and have them ask friends, to see if anyone has a margarita machine that can be brought for use at the party—making an extra-special drink for the bash makes your bar offerings list more impressive without spending a fortune.

• Sangria is the new, hot way to stretch your supply of wine—mixing a great red wine with fruit juice and fruit slices—and provide guests with a delicious, unique taste that's friendly on the wallet. Just have your co-hosts bring over their collections of glass pitchers, and you're all set to use drink recipes in sangria cookbooks and on Foodtv.com.

• Punches are back, big-time! Mix in just a bit of champagne or a liquor, and fill with your choice of juice and sorbet topper, ice ring, floating fruits, and other accents, and you get a budget-friendly crowd-pleaser in such flavors as pomegranate, apricot, peach, blackberry, orange, tropical fruit, and more. A single bottle of champagne plus fruit juices can provide enough drinks for twenty-four people, far more than the twelve people a bottle of wine supplies.

• For cultural drinks such as sake, plum wine, ouzo, and other liquors, buy or rent smaller sipping glasses—maybe smaller *but taller* shot glasses from Ikea or Pier 1—to allow you to treat your guests with just one bottle of the hard stuff.

• Look up seasonal drink recipes on Foodtv.com, and you may be able to DIY fabulously colored drinks that suit your theme and work with your low budget. For instance, a late fall, early-winter wedding would be fabulous with a spiked hot cider or hot toddy on the menu. With just a splash of liquor needed for each, your purchase of grocery store cider and simple DIY steps make it look like you spent way more.

• Ask your liquor store consultant to help you select moderately priced bar stock for multi-liquor drink ingredients (such as gin, triple sec, bitters, and other ingredients) that still wow the crowd but slice a percentage off your bar menu price tag. For single-liquor or on-the-rocks drinks—such as rum or vodka—stick with the quality brand names your crowd loves, to be sure all of your drinks taste top-shelf.

• Ask your bridesmaids to bring their own supply of *unopened* liquor bottles that they have in their bar cabinets as a freebie contribution to the party. Never let them drive around with bottles that have been opened and are screw-top capped, because getting pulled over by the police is always a possibility.

• For a coed party, beer is usually on the drinks list, so visit your local discount liquor store to stock up on a few cases of beer or micro-brews—and always ask the store manager if a discount is granted when you're buying so much. Most stores have existing policies to grant a price cut for bulk buys, and many managers are happy to grant you a great discount when you simply ask for one.

• Don't shop at the liquor departments in supermarkets you know to be pricey, just because it's conveniently near where you're buying some food items for the party. You'll pay 20 to 40 percent more than if you went to the liquor store as a separate errand.

• Skip the champagne as a solo drink for the toast. Leave that one to the bride and groom for their reception, and just let guests lift up whichever type of drink they have in front of them for any toasts proposed to the guest(s) of honor.

Non-Alcoholic Drinks

- Serve fabulous pitchers of iced tea in different flavors such as sweet tea, unsweetened, peach, berry, white tea, and more.

- Serve fabulous pitchers of lemonade in different flavors such as traditional, pink, and even a half-lemonade/half-iced tea blend.

- Mix up alcohol-free pitchers of sangria with grape juice, white grape juice, pomegranate and cranberry juice, and lots of fruit slices floating within.

- Make juice spritzers with two-thirds fruit juice and one-third seltzer or Sprite.

- Serve unique types of colas, such as cherry Coke, Dr. Pepper, orange soda, cream soda, root beer, birch beer, and other flavors that are close to standard cola cost but *look* like you spent more. And keep in mind that the presentation of soda can be a cost danger:

  - A six-pack of plastic Coke bottles costs $5.49 in my area.

  - A two-liter bottle of Coke costs $4.99.

  - A box of Coke cans with *double the ounces* than option #1 cost $2.50 in a 2-for-$5 sale!

  - Again, buy more than you'll need, and agree with your co-hosts that you'll bring home leftovers.

  - Look at the per-unit cost at discount warehouses to be sure that *name-brand* soda cases are truly a good deal. If you can get half the price per soda can, stock up!

- Don't forget to stock up on drink mixers, such as sodas, orange juice, pineapple juice, cranberry juice, and other bright beverages that also allow your liquor supply to stretch when guests make or request Bay Breezes or other island-style drinks. Supermarkets are often far better for buying these on your budget than liquor stores that often pump up their mixer prices.

- Water is in demand at parties! For an at-home party, just fill up pretty pitchers with some ice, filtered tap water, and drop in three or four slices of brightly colored lemons, limes, or oranges for a *free* crowd-pleaser.

Tap Water?

That's right . . . with a great faucet filter system like Pur or Brita, you can fill your pitchers with wonderfully fresh-tasting water in endless supply. At my own parties, I used to serve gallon after gallon of designer water, and my husband and I even had cases of it delivered every week for us to drink. We got used to it. But when I switched us to ice-cold filtered water with lemon, lime, orange, or cucumber slices, we *loved* it. We couldn't tell the difference, and we saved several dollars *per liter* by filling up our own pitcher regularly. So it's a great money-saver for your party, shaving a good $25 off of your party shopping list.

Coffee and Tea

I'm not going to tell you to buy the cheap stuff, because a great party is always going to get ruined when the last taste of the event is a bitter cup of coffee. Always shop for quality brands, preferably the kind you drink yourself, and get enough for each guest to enjoy two hot beverages at the close of the party.

I avoid buying my favorite Dunkin' Donuts coffee at the supermarket—where it's being stocked for convenience, in small bags, at high prices—and I shop at the Dunkin' Donuts store itself. At most DDs, they grant a discount when you buy two bags, and that turns into a nice savings.

And to ensure a great collection of teas, ask each of the co-host bridesmaids to bring a single, inexpensive box of flavored or decaf teabags. They can do the same with boxes of hot chocolate mix to create a budget-friendly hot cocoa bar, or borrow a friend's hot chocolate machine for a unique hot beverage at fall or winter showers. One can of whipped cream suits your crowd, and a baggie of marshmallows and a single chocolate bar to carve into topper shavings isn't going to dent your budget.

Of course, in order to serve these dishes and drinks, you'll need plenty of place settings. If your party will take place at a restaurant or hotel, it won't cost extra to use their standard patterns of dishes, bowls, glasses, and utensils, but you will be presented with a "menu" of upgraded styles, such as dishes in color, or intricate flatware. Skip these extra-pay designs and leave that styling to the bride.

How Many Drinks to Plan For

According to several bar managers, you should plan for guests to drink two drinks the first hour of the party, and then 1 drink each hour after that. Of course, that's a conservative estimate, since you may have guests who can down a glass of wine every ten minutes, and on a hot day your guests will drink more ice-cold drinks during the party. So do plan to get enough, without going overboard. Four to five drinks per person for a three-hour party is a good starting point. Or, you could use the fabulous *free* drink calculator at Evite.com. I plugged in the stats of a party that would last three hours, with twenty light drinkers and ten average drinkers, and the site told me to get six bottles of wine, a case of beer, and two bottles of liquor.

For an at-home party, you may be able to use your own dish and utensil collection, maybe borrow a collection or extras from other co-hosts, or rent your supplies as mentioned earlier. But if you'd like to shop for disposable plates and plastic cups to match the party's theme and colors, don't forget to comparison shop at stores like Target—where a big package of pink paper cups might be available for just a few dollars—in addition to party supply stores. Quality is always key, though, since you don't want cheap, floppy paper plates causing spill disasters along your buffet line when heavy foods cause those plates to lose their strength ... and staining foods hit the floor. Stick with brand names, check for coupons on those brand names at Coupons.com and other coupon sites, and see if solid-colored plates and cups will fit the bill in place of their pricey counterparts decorated with palm trees or hearts or other design elements.

CAKES AND DESSERTS

The perfect finale for your dazzling bridal shower is always going to be the desserts. You might have a sheet cake in traditional style, commission an artistic cake—say, in the shape of a shoe or of the bride's favorite book—or you might arrange a dessert buffet filled with pretty cupcakes and chocolate-covered berries. It's surprisingly affordable to create a fantastic dessert offering or bar, especially if you or anyone on your team can make the cake or cupcakes.

How Much Cake Do We Need?

The quickest way to overspend is to order too large a cake. Always go smaller than you think you'll need, since modest slices of cake will get a round or sheet cake to feed your guests amply. There always seems to be an insane amount of cake leftover at most parties . . . and you can only eat so much before throwing out a good chunk of it. Here are the sizes standard in the cake industry:

SIZE	SERVINGS
8"	10–14
9"	15–20
10"	22–27
12"	28–33
¼ SHEET	20–25
½ SINGLE SHEET	37–43
½ DOUBLE SHEET	45–50
FULL SINGLE SHEET	60–70
2 TIER: 10" AND 6"	35
2 TIER: 12" AND 8"	50
3 TIER: 12", 9", 6"	75

149

Now, on to your tips for saving money on your cake order:

• Order from the standard flavors list. These might be a yellow cake with lemon filling, a vanilla cake with buttercream filling and strawberries—the real crowd-pleasers. You'll spend extra—as much as $2 or more per slice!—if you order off the gourmet menu for rum cake or espresso cream-filled cake.

• Keep the cake décor simple, with just a basic icing cover and perhaps a few dots of icing to resemble pearls. When you ask for intricate piping and sugar-paste butterflies, the price skyrockets due to the extra labor.

• Fondant is often priced higher than regular icing, and some bakers have sworn off the artistic layer of smooth, thick icing in favor of the more popular (and some say tastier) whipped cream or butter-cream frosting.

• Negotiate out the cake-cutting fees if your party will be at a restaurant. Read the fine print of your contract to see if your site charges a per-slice plating fee that can sometimes be $1 or more *per slice served!* Most sites will be happy to strike that charge from your order if you ask.

• For two-tiered cakes, ask if your baker charges less to lay the top layer right on top of the bottom, rather than elevate it on pedestals (which is going out of style, anyway!).

• Choose just one flavor of filling for the cake. If you and the group were to ask for three different fillings on each layer, that baker's going to charge more for the extra work.

• Ask a talented friend or relative to make a simple sheet cake with minimal design, and reimburse her if you require her to buy a heart-shaped cake pan to suit your party's theme. Again, the cake can be her gift to the bride!

• Check out the prices of sheet cakes at your supermarket, which might be less than what the local bakery charges. Your habit of going right to the bakery could cost you 20 percent or more than you might otherwise spend.

• Check out the prices of sheet cakes at stores like Costco and Sam's Club, and ask the baker there if you can get a taste sample before you order.

Some discount cakes can be too sugary sweet, so if they use the same batter for their cupcakes as for their cakes, the baker can give you a bite.

Cupcakes

• This one is an easy group DIY project! Perhaps your co-hosts can come over the day before to make the cupcakes, and then you'll all spend a few hours earlier in the day giving them a fresh coat of frosting and décor.

• If getting together is a challenge, perhaps each of you can bake a single batch of cupcakes and decorate with pastel-colored frostings, then bring your batches to the party. The cost to you: under $7 in most cases, less with a coupon!

• Borrow a friend's cupcake tree (a multi-tiered display stand for cupcakes) rather than buying one.

• Visit the craft store to stock up on cute cupcake papers in different colors, or suiting your theme, for less than if you bought those multitonal collections at the supermarket.

• Top cupcakes with bulk-buy candies such as jelly beans in pastel colors, only the yellow M&Ms from a huge bag you bought at Costco (a savings over ordering custom-color M&M bags online—they're quite pricey!), or crumbled Oreo cookies, to name a few.

• Copy gourmet cupcake creations and hold a stencil (heart-shaped, star-shaped, letter-shaped, etc, from the craft store) over each cupcake, carefully sprinkle on a light dusting of cocoa powder, confectioner's sugar, or cinnamon, lift the stencil up, and voilà! Your gourmet cupcakes are ready. And you spent $2, instead of $40 for a dozen.

Additional Desserts

Tops on the DIY dessert list for a beautiful buffet of desserts are:

• Brownie squares

• Cheesecake squares

• Carrot cake squares

- Blocks of fudge

- Chocolate-dipped fruits

- Cookie platter, with chocolate chip cookies, macadamia nut cookies, peanut butter cookies, and more to give a selection

- If you'd rather buy brownies and the like, platters found at Costco are the top choice, often priced extremely well for a tray that feeds your entire guest list. Coming in second is the supermarket bakery platters, also a great buy.

Time It Right for Freebies

"My supermarket's Sunday circular has been offering a great coupon for $20 off if you spend over $75. So I combined my own weekly shopping list with my pickups for the party, and I got the brownie tray for *free*! Just for shopping for things I needed anyway."

—CAROL, RECENT BRIDESMAID FROM GEORGIA

- Ask a mom, grandmom, or other special relative to whip up a batch of the bride's favorite dessert, such as her mom's chocolate mousse. Just one batch is fine to feed the guest list.

- For fruit platters—which are always popular, but can run up your food budget when organic fruits are priced high—make a smaller platter more fascinating by DIYing your collection into creative cuts of tropical fruits, Mandarin oranges, single packs of blueberries and raspberries, and other sweet, natural treats. Use small cookie cutters to make star- or heart-shapes or circles out of slices of cantaloupe and honeydew for a special touch that costs nothing when you own or borrow the cutters.

- Don't buy the precut fruit bowls from the supermarket, which can cost more than twice the price of taking the time to wash and cut the fruit yourself.

BRIDESMAID ON A BUDGET

• Create a fabulous presentation of fruits by making kebobs with them; the arrangement actually makes it look like you have far more fruit in your supply.

• Fruits are fine when served without dipping sauces, so no need to spend extra on those pricey jars of fruit dips. Or, DIY with fruit dip recipes at FoodTV.com.

• Petits fours are traditional bridal shower bites, but their intricate formation means higher prices at the cash register. Just get one pack of a dozen at the supermarket as an accent to a dessert platter, rather than buying enough for each guest to have three.

• An ice cream bar is a waste of money, since guests tend to eat sparingly when it comes to desserts. Those big tubs of three different flavors are surely going to melt and go to waste. Plus, assembling all the toppings can add up to big expense. Leave this one to the bride's own parties.

• Create your own trendy dessert bar with bowls filled with different colors of jelly beans or different chocolates, and let guests scoop their choices into ultra-inexpensive baggies from the craft store. Supply them with twist-ties to keep their baggies closed—at least until they can start snacking during the drive home!

• Don't go crazy with the desserts! Just two or three fabulous options will be a thrill to your guests.

Remember that presentation makes everything look pricier, so get out that silver platter, that fabulous tray from your mom's house, a crystal bowl, an authentic Tuscan bowl, and set your inexpensive desserts on top of those . . . spaced with some fresh strawberries, just the way they present desserts in restaurants. It makes a great impression . . . for *free*.

Finally, as much as it sounds like it would be a great idea to have guests take home dessert bar leftovers as their favors, it's a classier touch to hold aside a collection of bagged cookies or candies—items that would have been on the favor bar—for them to take home. It still saves money, but it just looks more planned, and it keeps the snacks safely sealed and germ-free in their separate display.

Sometimes You Just Have to Splurge

"We live right near the bakery where *Cake Boss* is filmed, and I know the bride loves the desserts from there," says one recent bridesmaid from Hoboken, New Jersey. "So the other bridesmaids and I cut out a few little things from the budget so that we could splurge and get her an amazing, gooey chocolate mousse cake from that bakery. She *loved* it. And the guests were really impressed that they got to taste some 'celebrity' cake." If there's a big-ticket dessert item you know the bride would love, clear some space in the budget to make that happen for her, as well. A single splurge can make your party shine.

CHAPTER 11

Planning the Bridal Shower—
Favors and Prizes

*T*hese are the goodies you'll give out at the shower . . . those fantastic favors that guests are glad to have, and the fun prizes they win by participating in the games you've planned. If you have a sizeable guest list, you're likely concerned about what it will cost to buy so many favors, plus fantastic prizes, that will impress.

Let's get right to a new trend that can save you a fortune: Some shower hosts are *skipping the games*. That's right . . . no clothespin game. No "what's in your purse" checklists rewarding the person with the most stuff in her handbag. No trivia questions about the couple. Some brides who hated having to sit through the game hour at other showers insist that no games be planned for their own showers. So that means you won't have to spend money on game supplies, nor prizes. That's a good $75 back in your pockets, depending on your penchant for pricey prizes.

"At a recent bridal shower I attended, the bridal party gave out huge baskets of spa supplies from an ultra-expensive designer brand, and while the winners gushed, you could tell the bridesmaids hated shelling out so much for these prizes," says one shower guest from San Francisco.

Your favors and prizes can thrill your guests, even at low, low prices. Here's how. . . .

FAVORS

Your goal is to give a favor that's a real treat and perhaps even offers guests their *choices* of items, such as at a candy or cookie bar where they select their own favorite flavors and package their own take-homes. Speaking of treats, let's start with the most popular choice in favors. . . .

Edibles

These are the snacks that most guests finish off in the car before they get home, with most costing less than $1 each as batches are divided up, bagged or boxed, and presented as favors.

- Chocolate chip cookies, either old-school or gourmet, such as with white chocolate chips, macadamia nuts, and other add-ins

- Oatmeal raisin cookies

- Frosted sugar cookies, with shower theme-color frosting

- Baggies of M&Ms, jelly beans, or other popular candies

- Baggies of retro candies like Sweethearts, Red Hots, Mary Janes, and Gobstoppers

- Brownies

- Blondies

- Cupcakes, either regular-sized or minis

- Spice bars or pumpkin bars for fall-themed parties

- Caramel apple on a stick, bagged—as a fabulous DIY project, dip these in chocolate chips, crushed nuts, sprinkles, or other fabulous treats

- Girl Scout cookies, with guests' choice of different flavors (and a very happy Girl Scout to have sold you a dozen boxes!)

- Homemade truffles

- Homemade chocolates, made from choco-molding kits bought at the craft store

- Baggies of unique veggie snacks such as wasabi peas and dried banana chips

- Jar of salsa, giving guests their choice of mild, medium, or smokin' hot

- Gourmet lollipops

- Flavored marshmallow squares

- Rice Krispie Treat super-squares dipped in white chocolate and chocolate chips (Make your own, to emulate the Godiva treat for far less!)

Package It Up

Presentation is key, so pick a great way to package favors. Tie with a ribbon that you've curled at the ends. Your local craft store will have a fantastic array of inexpensive favor baggies and favor boxes, or you could shop at BayleysBoxes.com to get budget-friendly favor boxes in the shapes of stars, flowers, hearts, and in fabulous colors and patterns. Tag favors with a note thanking guests for coming and wishing them a sweet ride home.

Pampering Products

Give guests a small indulgence with these $2-and-under items:

- Small bottles of Bath & Body Works lotions, bath oils, and lip balms

- Burts Bees regular or tinted lip balms

- Bubble baths

- Bath salts or bath bombs

- Small packets of rose petals with a note to sprinkle in the bathtub

Charitables

Follow the bride's lead and have your big party give a little back, in the form of arranging for charitable favors. Print out pretty cards letting guests know that a donation has been made to the bride's favorite charity in lieu of favors. You and the other shower hosts can agree on a cause, write a check for a moderate amount, and keep the amount quiet. There's no need to try to impress guests by printing out a card saying you gave $200. "We know the bride loves animals, so we made a donation to the nearby zoo!" says one bridesmaid from New Jersey. "And she got a certificate announcing her 'share' of ownership in the wolves that live there. She *loved* it!" The charity can be local, national, or international. Just be sure to stick with a legitimate charity that you've known about for a long time, and check them out at www.give.org to be sure you're not being scammed. Here are some ways to save even more on charitable favors:

- Print out four to six announcement cards to each sheet of heavier-grade paper, rather than spending more on perforated "postcard" sheets at the office supply store, and cut the squares yourself.

- Use colored ink on your announcements to add visual appeal, plus a scroll or monogram on top, and you won't need to decorate the cards any further, such as with ribbon bows or other accents.

- Many charities offer these favor announcement cards for *free*, so be sure to ask or check the website carefully to find out if you can get your cards gratis.

- Display your donation announcement sign in a frame you already own.

- Leave these cards at each table place setting instead of buying a display platter.

- Attach a small, wrapped candy to each announcement card, with a $3 bag of candies fulfilling the job.

Print Items

Visit the bookstore or DIY your own handy print items:

- Bookmarks
- Magnetic notepads from the $1 bin at the craft store or Target
- Notepads from the $1 bin at the craft store or Target
- A romantic quote you've printed out on parchment or colored paper, and inserted into a $1.99 magnetic frame from the craft store

What About the Guys?

For coed showers, edible favors are always a winning choice on the cheap.

GAME PRIZES WORTH WINNING

No matter what the game is, the winner loves being named the victor with the prize basket being handed to her. Here is where you make the winner beam while still protecting your wallet. I've broken these down by *shower theme*, in case you'd like to match the prize to the style of your party. (Of course, all are up for grabs if you don't have a shower theme, and all work as favors, too!) All prizes are under $10 each:

Kitchen Theme

- A jar of gourmet salsa
- A bottle of fabulous sauce, perhaps from a celebrity chef's line
- A magnet set for the fridge
- A small cookbook from the bookstore's bargain shelves at under $7, often themed such as "Cupcakes" or "Cookies" or "Sangria."

- A small pot of herbs, such as rosemary or thyme, or a potted "kitchen garden" with basil, parsley, chives, and other herbs

- A cute, basic silver trivet or trio of trivets

- A newly released cookbook from your favorite celebrity chef

- The newest issue of a fabulous gourmet magazine

Island Theme (for a pre-destination wedding shower)

- Piña colada mix

- Daiquiri mix

- A container of macadamia nuts

- A small bottle of rum, such as Mount Gay or Cruzan

- A cute beach towel

- A travel journal

- A travel alarm clock

- Cute luggage tags

- A themed key chain, sporting flip-flops, sunglasses, or other beachy icons

- An underwater one-time-use camera that the winner can use during her next island getaway or just in the backyard pool

- A CD of steel drum music or island tunes

- A cookbook themed to the destination wedding location

- An issue of *Budget Traveler* or other fabulous travel magazine

- A passport cover, in a fun and funky plastic design

Garden Theme

- Cute gardening gloves

- A padded kneeling cushion in the shape of a daisy

- Packets of wildflower or lavender seeds

- A potted Gerber daisy in a bright color

- An issue of an unusual gardening magazine (since many guests may already subscribe to the most popular ones)

- A book on container gardening or other floral topic from the bookstore's bargain rack

- A décor stone with a word imprinted on it, such as *Peace, Goodness, Hope*, or another sentiment

- A book on identifying local birds—one of the most popular prizes out there, since families find that they love sharing their downtime spotting birds in their yards and getting excited about seeing a new type of bird!

Wine Lovers

- Coasters

- A bottle of great wine

- A wine journal

- A chill bucket

- Wine bottle stoppers in cute designs

- Wine charm sets

- An issue of a wine appreciation magazine

- Cheese boards with cheese picks or cheese knives

- A book on wine-growing regions of the world

- A pair of great wineglasses, perhaps with colored stems, from Crate and Barrel, Ikea, or other super-affordable stores

Non-Theme Shower Prizes

- Cute Post-It notes in flower shapes and bright colors

- Magnetic notepads for the refrigerator or side of a filing cabinet

- Organizing baskets in different sizes

- Notecard boxes

- Clusters of fine-point pens in different colors (in keeping with everyone's wish to be more organized)

- Potted plants such as fern, succulents, tiny bamboo shoots, and more

- Single-stem roses or bunches of tulips

It's Not under $10, But . . .

One of the hottest shower game prizes out there is the $15 iTunes gift card that your guests can use to upload music, podcasts, and more.

CHAPTER 12

Planning the Bridal Shower—Your Gift

*G*et ready to smile . . . it's a fabulous, new trend out there for lovely, considerate brides to insist that throwing a bridal shower *is* their gift! Some brides refuse to accept any additional presents, being wonderfully mindful of the wallop their maids' wallets take in planning a party for twenty, forty, or more guests. So *if* the bride says, "No gifts, ladies," you can count yourself among the lucky bridesmaids out there who get a bit of a break. Indeed, the *experience* of a fabulous bridal shower shared with all of the bride's friends and family is the best present possible.

And here's the next happy trend: More bridesmaid groups are going in on group gifts, getting that $200 cookware set or that $200 bedding set, and splitting the cost five or more ways. The bride and groom get a much-wanted gift they really need, and you only spend $30 or $40. That's way better on your budget since it delivers a fabulous gift, and you don't feel the need to spend $100 on something more impressive and special for the dear bride.

The Most Common Group Gifts for the Bride

According to TheWeddingReport.com, these big-ticket items are among the most popular choices for bridal shower gifts co-given and co-paid by the bridesmaids:

- Cookware

- Dinnerware, the complete set

- Silverware collections, the complete set

- Espresso machine

- Coffeemaker with grinder

- Microwave

- Stand mixer

- Bedding set

- Towels, the complete set

- Vacuum, the *good* one with the allergen setting

- Luggage set

Another fun group gift is joining together to get something from the couple's honeymoon registry—such as a limousine ride from the airport to the hotel, a couple's massage on the beach, a romantic sunset dinner, a swim with dolphins. Or, they give the couple a sizeable gift card to their honeymoon resort so that they can book whichever adventure, spa service, or romantic meal they desire. A $200 gift card from the bridesmaids, again, could only cost you $40 or less.

Here's a chart that shows what you would spend as part of a group gift:

YOUR EXPENSE				
	GROUP OF 4	GROUP OF 5	GROUP OF 6	GROUP OF 8
$100 GIFT	$25	$20	$16	$12.50
$200 GIFT	$50	$40	$33	$25
$300 GIFT	$75	$60	$50	$37.50
$400 GIFT	$100	$80	$66	$50

WHAT IF THE GROUP WANTS TO GET THEIR OWN, INDIVIDUAL GIFTS?

Some bridesmaids don't like the idea of going in on a group gift. Maybe they've already purchased something from the registry, or maybe they have a different gift in mind. This doesn't mean the option is out.

You can split the cost of a gift with another bridesmaid . . . or even with non-bridesmaids. There's no circle drawn around the group of bridesmaids, requiring you to only co-gift with them. Ask other friends, colleagues, or relatives if they'd like to go in with you on that cookware set or the espresso maker. This might even add up to *ten* contributors, cutting your share down even more! Get creative, and think about who might be willing to join you in a group gift. With more than five people in your group, though, it's a great idea to "dress up" your gift with a few little extras in your presentation—such as a cookbook to go with the cookware set, or a $12 set of espresso cups and saucers from the registry.

GIFT CARDS THAT THRILL

Whether in a group or on your own, a gift card to the bride's registry lets her stock up on all of the essentials that she and the groom need for their new home. And your gift card—even a modest one—can help her get that amazing luggage set she wants, a coffeemaker, her towels, a duvet cover, or her sheets set.

Don't forget that gift cards don't have to be from the registry. Your fabulous, budget-friendly gift could be a gift card to the beauty salon where she'll get her wedding hair and makeup done…or she can use it for a relaxing mani-pedi next week! A gift card to the couple's favorite restaurant lets them have a date night on the cheap, since they have so many expenses right now, as well.

If you know the bride and groom are working on their home, a gift card to Home Depot or Lowes is beyond thrilling for many wedding couples, who are now one step closer to being able to paint their bedroom. If you know that they're saving up to get a fabulous new television, you may choose to arrange a group-contribution to a gift card through stores like Best Buy that have new programs allowing for special occasion big-ticket presents.

Go to the Jungle

Again, at PlasticJungle.com, you might be able to buy a gift card that someone else has traded in for less than face value. So a fully loaded $100 gift card to the registry might only cost you $60. Allow plenty of time for order and delivery, since it can take weeks for the card to arrive.

THE MODEST SHOWER GIFT

Remember, the average bridal shower gift bought by an individual bridesmaid, according to TheWeddingReport.com, costs $72. You can cut that by *two-thirds* and still thrill the bride when you get her one of the items from her registry that she's going to *love* and use often. It might be that set of coffee mugs she signed on for at $20 for a set of four. She'll use one of those coffee mugs every morning, and she'll remember your note about how often the two of you would sit out on your porch, drinking coffee, discussing your adventures in singles world. Or you'll get her that $20 set of margarita glasses with a framed photo of the two of you in Cancun, toasting to the camera during your fabulous girls' getaway last year.

When you mix in a touch of sentimentality with a photo, even a $9.99 item off of her registry becomes one of her favorite gifts.

Great Gifts for Under $50 . . . and Under $25

You can get a fabulous gift from the top bridal registries for under $50, or even under $25, by clicking on the registry's Gifts page and requesting to see their suggested gifts—broken down into such categories as "For the Home" and "For the Garden"—in your choice of budget range. I logged onto Bed Bath & Beyond and Crate and Barrel to see what I might be able to get for under $50, and also for under $25. Looking for impressive gifts that don't look cheap, I found a treasure trove of fabulous possibilities:

BED BATH & BEYOND, UNDER $25

- Omelette pan
- Crepe pan
- Double boiler
- Bamboo steamer
- Crème brûlée torch set

BED BATH & BEYOND, $25 TO $50

- Calphalon omelette pan
- Wok set
- Paella pan
- Pancake pan
- Spice grinder
- Steamer
- Ice cream maker

- Hamilton Beach drink mixer
- Cheese board sets

CRATE AND BARREL, UNDER $25

- Cocktail shaker
- 12 appetizer plates
- Glass pitcher
- Cheese dome
- Wine carafe
- Glass teapot
- Galvanized party tub
- Pizza board
- Frother

I didn't even look at the higher-priced gifts from Crate and Barrel, since this list was so pleasing. I include these here not as your shopping list, but as a glimpse into the kinds of items that might already be on the couple's registry. That cheese board collection could be your early pick and quick snap-up for the ideal, solo shower gift. So *shop early* . . . since many of the couple's friends and family members are going right to the registry today to grab those same moderately priced gifts way in advance of the shower! The early bird gets the great budget gift!

The Gift That Keeps on Coming

I love giving magazine subscriptions as bridal shower gifts! They arrive each month with fresh ideas, recipes, organization tips, travel ideas … all of the fun stuff a newlywed couple loves. And these days, subscriptions can cost as low as $10 for a year! And when you renew your own subscriptions, you may be offered a free gift subscription to give to someone else, which makes your gift free. Package a few issues of the magazine in a basket, add some recipe cards for a gourmet magazine or a bottle of sunscreen with a travel magazine, and you're all set for under $15.

DAZZLING DIY GIFTS

The Do-It-Yourself trend in wedding planning extends to your shower plans, with your craft talents making a fabulous, inexpensive gift possible. Here's how today's bridesmaids are making gifts for the bride for under $20:

• If you have a side business making charm bracelets, create one for the bride using charms and supplies you already own.

• Create a travel journal for the bride, taking a regular under-$5 journal found in the bookstore and personalizing it with your handwritten quotes about travel and adventure on the tops of some pages. You invest under an hour, and your $5 gift looks like you spent $30 or more.

• Make a personalized collection of wine charms stamped with images or words that mean a lot to the bride.

• Personalize table place mats, including iron-on kits to allow you to decorate linen placements with your choice of images or words.

• Take a pretty piece of wood with beveled edges, and carefully hand-paint the bride's favorite quote or a line from her favorite book or movie . . . or use a décor-perfect phrase, such as *And they lived happily ever after* or *The best is yet to be.*

It Doesn't Have to Be Your DIY!

Just because it's handmade doesn't mean it has to be your hands that made it. Visit church craft fairs, street festivals, and fairs where enterprising crafters display their goods for sale. You may find just those kinds of hand-painted signs—made with excellent skill using the Cricut Express—for under $20 apiece. Check out Etsy.com for low-priced, pretty crafts—and again, some Etsy crafts are pretty pricey, so shop well!

WHAT ABOUT THE WEDDING GIFT?

It's not proper etiquette for the bridal party to go in on a group gift for this one. So this is one area where it's not wise to look for ways to save. Just give a gift that's in keeping with your family and regional "usual amounts," and if it's your circle's practice to give wrapped gifts rather than cash- or check-stuffed envelopes, choose something wonderful and meaningful from the wedding registry. Get two of the couple's wished-for champagne flutes and package them in a basket with a fabulous champagne or bottle of wine, with a note requesting that they use this gift to celebrate their return home after the wedding. The cost? Under $75 in many cases, when you choose a fantastic bottle of champagne as recommended to you by the expert at your local liquor shop, or through a search of best-rated, moderately priced champagnes on WineSpectator.com or FoodandWine.com.

If you're going to house sit for the couple while they're away on their honeymoon—or if you know the person who will be house sitting—you might stock their refrigerator with fantastic meals from their favorite restaurant, fresh milk, and other essentials and treats such as a chocolate cake, so that they don't have to go food shopping the night they return. Your note to them invites them to stay in, cocoon, and enjoy these meals and indulgences that you've chosen especially for them. With a bouquet of fresh flowers on their table, your gift may cost under $80. And they'll *love* it.

On a lower-budget, welcome home theme, leave on their table a collection of the photos you and some other friends took at the wedding, plus the edit you made of some video that a friend took for them, as well. And a bottle of wine. The cost: under $30.

CHAPTER 13

Bachelorette Party Expenses

*F*ollow the advice in the previous chapters to help you save a fortune on any food, drinks, and décor for the bachelorette party you're hosting, and look to this chapter to help you design and host a bachelorette bash the bride will love. Now before you take one step, *make sure the bride wants to have a bachelorette party*.

Some brides don't want them at all, wishing to save their bridesmaids the expense, and it might be that the distance between the bride and all of the bridesmaids and friends is too great to make the scheduling of *another* party realistic. If the bride will only arrive in town for the wedding a few days prior to the Big Day, there may not be time for a bachelorette party. She has too much else to do, and the bridal shower is taking place a few days before the wedding. So plans for a bachelorette party are out the window.

For the brides who *do* want a bachelorette bash, the *style* of party determines the budget. Will it be:

A. The traditional club-hopping drinkfest with the bride wearing an attention-getting puff veil and a T-shirt inviting guys to bite candy off her chest. OR

B. A more upscale, elegant cocktail party, a brunch, a girls' day at the salon, a girls' day at the beach, or other alternative bachelorette party plan.

"I Didn't Miss It at All"

"I didn't want a bachelorette party, since my bridesmaids and friends were going to be driving into town the day before the wedding from three states away—each of them taking a day off of work and paying for two nights in the hotel already. I could never ask them to take off another day, or drive hours out here the weekend before the wedding, so I decided just to grab two hours with them on the morning of the rehearsal. We had a champagne breakfast at my house, and then we went for a walk through my neighborhood, where all the cherry trees were in bloom and it was raining tiny flower petals. We got to catch up, have some laughs, take some fabulous photos of us under the cherry trees, and just have a great morning together before I had to run off and get lots of last-minute things done. It was perfect!"

—ALICIA, RECENT BRIDE FROM NEW JERSEY

The maid of honor will lead the way in the planning, after consulting with the bride about her wishes or just *knowing* that the bride would hate a raunchy party with male dancers and drunken guests spilling out of the limo, and someone having to have their hair held back at the end of the night while someone else holds a champagne bucket. With the maid of honor in charge, letting you know the style the party will be, here are some ideas to cut down the costs of *any* type of bachelorette party:

• Limit the guest list. Not every female wedding guest needs to be invited, even though everyone wants to make the A-list. Just super-close friends of the bride, and the bridesmaids. For tamer parties, sometimes the moms and fun grandmas are invited, too!

• Use Evite, your free invitations tool that lets you all keep track of RSVPs.

• For the at-home portion of the party, where guests will enjoy a cocktail party and appetizers, follow the menu and drinks advice in Chapter 10.

• Talk with the maid of honor to be clear on who's splitting the bill out at a restaurant or bar. Will you go traditional with the hosts (you and the bridesmaids) picking up the tab? That's the most etiquette-correct plan, although the group may agree on their own to share costs. Be sure to pre-arrange the pay plan, since you don't want your credit card—handed to the barkeep to run your tab—to get walloped with a huge bill, and then have you chasing down co-planners for weeks to get them to pay their share.

• Arrange for safe transportation if your party will be a bar-hopping extravaganza. Many groups arrange to split the cost of a limousine for a ride in style that allows everyone to partake in champagne toasts or other drinks along the way. Ask friends who they hired as their special event limousines, and ask if they offer special discount rates for bachelorette party groups. Some limo companies out there—in competition with other local companies—often provide bachelorette-bash packages for less than the three-hour bridal package.

• For a larger group of planners to split the bill, check out the costs of a party bus that also delivers you to each stop along the way in a club-like atmosphere on wheels. Ask about budget packages, and perhaps even a two-hour bus booking rather than the far more expensive all-night ride.

• If a co-planner or friend doesn't mind being the Designated Driver, you have no transportation costs. A great gesture is to give the sober-driving bridesmaid a price break on her share of the bachelorette party expenses, since she is doing everyone a huge favor. And if it's *you* passing up the body shots as the DD, you get to claim that discount.

• Have the party in a location that requires no driven transportation, such as getting a private area in the hotel's own nightclub. As part of a wedding party, you might be granted a big discount for giving the hotel your business. Ask what can be arranged, and you may save hundreds of dollars for your group.

• If you'll plan a girls' getaway for the bachelorette party, use every travel discount at your disposal to get great flight rates and hotel rooms, and then you can enjoy Vegas or any vacation spot at fabulous discounts. Think about it: If you can book a hotel suite at a resort area an hour or two away for $150, that means you won't have to pay over $200 for a limo to take you all around to the local hotspots in your hometown. A short drive with the girls, then, saves you a bundle and lets you allow your favorite nearby vacation locale as your official bachelorette getaway overnighter.

• Keep the getaway to just an overnight to keep it affordable for you and for other guests. A three-day stay is fine for those bridal groups who have a lot more money to spend.

• Skip the cliché bachelorette party favors like the penis-shaped lol-lipops and tiaras, the feather boa for the bride, and all other tired-trend add-ons that just aren't necessary and that can seem too raunchy for some guests.

• If you'll plan a girls' day at the spa, check a few different top-name spas and salons in your area to compare their price packages for group events. And look beyond the packages titled "Bachelorette" or "Bridal," since they can sometimes be hoisted in price due to their special nature. Just research the packages for a simple "group party" instead. You get the same manicures, pedicures, hot stone massages, and facials for 20 percent less, in some cases.

Entertainment

• Skip the male dancers. The bride can live without the oiled-up mus-cleman gyrating in front of her face.

• Edit a fun slideshow of photos you have of the bride, using your home computer's movie-maker software—or ask a talented friend to take this on—and produce a funny tribute video to the bride, such as all of her hair-cuts through the years.

• Hook up that iPod for your own fabulous playlist at your at-home party.

• Turn on the TV to host a viewing of the newest release movies that are on your For-Pay movie channel, and everyone can slumber-party-style with a movie marathon for under $5 per movie, plus a menu of snacks and margaritas.

• Ask friends to bring their newly acquired, hot-title DVDs for your movie night.

• Arrange *no* entertainment, and just let friends who haven't seen each other in a long time catch up without enforced group fun, games, and movie viewing. These relaxed cocktail parties are often the biggest hits!

• *Be* the entertainment! Out at a club, your bride wearing that poof tiara is going to attract a lot of attention, and—let's face it—guys buy drinks for groups of bachelorettes. Even the bar may give you a free round or two so that you love them and come back to their place for the next bachelorette party you plan. The savings can add up tremendously when you're getting free rounds from well-wishers.

What If You're Far from the Party?

Q: *I live over twelve hours away from where they're having the shower, and with the expenses of the dress and my travel and hotel for the wedding, I am just not going to be able to make it to the bachelorette party. Do I have to pay for a share of it even without my being there?*

A: No, you don't. While some maids of honor may ask you to pay your share so that you can be listed as a party host, that's not up to her. It's up to you. You don't have to split the bill for a party you won't attend. But it *is* nice to send a small amount to help the group pay for a great time for the bride.

Some additional ways to save:

• Skip the decorated bride's T-shirts that you see on the rack at bridal salons. They're often way overpriced, with some at $40 or more. Instead, shop at CafePress.com to get a wide range of Bride and Bridesmaid T-shirts, if you'd like, for under $20 apiece.

• Say no to the matching bridesmaid T-shirts, which some bridesmaids may want to get attention at the clubs. Just tell them you'd rather wear something stylish and sexy, since you'll be out among eligible men.

• Skip the theme napkins and coasters, and just get plain, solid-colored ones at the party supply store, dollar store, or Target for far less than themed partyware.

• Favors are *not* necessary for a bachelorette party. The take-home for guests are memories of a great party.

• If you absolutely must have an X-rated cake, it's better to make one yourself rather than pay top dollar at a baker . . . and it's less embarrassing, too. Ask friends if they have or can borrow any theme shape cake pans, or just do some fancy cake shaping with a plain, old sheet cake or round cake you make yourself. Store-bought theme cake: $50 or more. DIY theme cake: under $10.

If you'll host an at-home bachelorette party, ask if the other bridesmaids can bring over a few of the bottles of wine they have sitting in their wine racks, but not too old and still drinkable. Each bottle that comes in saves you $15 or so.

What About Parties Hosted by Others?

These days, a bridesmaid is invited to two or three bridal showers for the bride, *in addition* to the one she's co-hosting. Since our global society often has friends, relatives, and colleagues of the bride (and groom) scattered far and wide, different regional groups often choose to throw a bridal shower for the happy couple. And it's a point of good etiquette for the hosts to invite all of the bridesmaids.

The good news is that you don't have to go to all of them. The close ones that are easy to get to, you may certainly attend if you wish. It's great manners if you do. But for those long-distance ones, the ones that require a pricey plane or train ticket or hours spent driving, it's okay to send your regrets.

If you do attend any additional bridal showers, it's considered proper for you to bring a gift to each one, even if you hosted the primary bridal shower and gave a gift at that one. No need to buy a pricey gift to stay on pace with the other guests; just a simple, smaller gift from the registry or a gift card to the registry is perfectly acceptable in the bride's eyes, and thus for your wallet.

All additional wedding weekend events, like an after-party or day-after event, are completely at your discretion to attend or not attend. It's quite common for bridal party members to check out of their hotels the next morning and head back home, free as they are to skip any additional events planned by the bride's and groom's families, such as barbecues and family softball games. Again, your obligations as a great bridesmaid are done, and there is absolutely no rule saying you have to shell out for another night's stay at the hotel if that's beyond your budget. Stay and play, or leave and save. It's your call.

Part Three

Unexpected
Expenses

CHAPTER 14

Travel and Transportation Extras for Destination Weddings

hen it's announced that this will be a destination wedding you'll be attending, you might break out into a cold sweat over how much more this could potentially cost you. After all, you know that a few days' stay at a fabulous resort can easily cost a few thousand dollars, and airfare, too, can drain away several hundred dollars ... depending on where you're going.

Some brides and grooms may pick up everyone's travel and lodging tabs as part of a resort's sweet discount deal for a group of ten or so guests. At an all-inclusive resort, where all food and drinks are included, that great group rate could be the smartest decision they've made during all their time together thus far. For the average destination wedding cost of just over $7,000—far less than the national wedding cost average of over $20,000—they and their guests enjoy an exotic, tropical, adventurous, and indulgent dream getaway wedding weekend in paradise.

Or, the destination wedding might not be located on an island, overseas, or anyplace requiring plane travel. A new trend is for the destination wedding to take place just a few hours away, at a fabulous tourist area or a ski resort the couple has frequented, or that their family has traditionally visited each year, so airfare won't be necessary at all.

No matter where your group is headed, here are some smart ways to stick to your budget and save:

• Ask the bride and groom if the group will be locked into an all-inclusive rate, or if everyone gets to choose their own meal plans. Here's why: At some resorts, the all-inclusive rates could be divided by your number of days on-location to reveal a $75 per day food and drink expense. Will you actually eat and drink $75 worth? During our recent honeymoon, we wound up switching our meal plan because we weren't coming anywhere near $75 apiece per day. So being able to pay as we went saved us over 45 percent. You might be able to customize your plan for smarter spending, so ask the bride what the arrangements are and if you can switch off of the all-inclusive plan. Many wedding guests who are not big drinkers, who prefer an iced tea over a Long Island iced tea, choose this path. And many guests who plan to down frozen, liquored-up drinks from noon to sunrise—with each drink at $15 apiece—find the all-inclusive to be a *huge* savings. Do your own math and potentially save a bundle.

• Another thing to consider about all-inclusive meal plans: Will you eat every meal on the resort grounds, or will your group venture out into the towns for authentic cuisine? When you're on an all-inclusive, you'll still pay for the meal you're not having back at the hotel while you're paying for this fabulous other meal out on the town or out at a festival.

• Ask if hotel transfers are included. This is one that many brides and grooms don't know offhand or haven't looked into, but some resorts will charge $10 to $15 per guest for the ride or ferry to the resort from the airport. It might be in the small print that this charge is *not* in the group plan, so check the fine print carefully. Most resorts do cater to wedding groups by including such details or by making them free, but this is one of those little surprise expenses that the occasional resort will leave out there for the paying. Check with the bride to see if she's looked into this, and she can ask her coordinator to arrange a freebie for her guests.

• If it's early enough to make suggestions to the wedding couple, see if it's okay for four or five or you to share a villa or suite at the resort. The bride and groom might be inspired by your suggestion and request a special bridal group discount for *that* room, as well. You save and land a fun group stay in a luxury villa with your own horizon pool and a great view.

• Suggest to the bride and groom that they look into group airfare deals, as mentioned earlier in this book. Destination wedding packages are sometimes *linked* by the resort to an airline's special wedding group rates, yours for the asking.

• Ask the bride if she's arranging for hair and makeup services at the resort, and if you'll be expected to pay for those. Never assume that every expense will be covered, even if it's something you would do for your own destination wedding guests. Bridesmaids who assume might get stunned with a fresh charge to sign to their room.

• Don't worry about buying all new dresses and shoes to wear to the rehearsal dinner and other dress-up occasions. Bring your own, and you'll look fantastic.

• Limit your souvenir shopping. Remember that gift shop prices are often sky-high, and many brides and grooms surprise their guests with goodie bags containing take-home T-shirts and souvenirs upon departure. Money saved: over $50.

• Check the hotel website to see which amenities are free, such as biking, kayaking, and tennis, and plan on *those* for your "bachelorette party" with all guests present during the big weekend.

• Another option for your bachelorette party is the *free* afternoon High Tea that many resorts offer, with a fabulous buffet of finger sandwiches, tea cakes, and cookies to go with iced and hot teas.

• And yet another free option for your hosted weekend event for the girls or as a coed party is the resort's free stargazing event or guided nature tours.

• Beware of roaming charges with your phone from that location. Don't get shocked with a big bill when you return home. Many resorts have office centers at which you can upload pictures and updates to your Facebook page without having to pay per-text fees. The savings here: up to $100 if you're really into sharing details from the weekend with those back home.

CHAPTER 15

Photos and Video

There's no need to hire a professional photographer or videographer for the bridal shower, since you and others can use your terrific digital cameras and Flip video cameras to capture all the best moments of the celebration. You can then edit out the bad shots, retake some photos, and upload your images and video right to sharing sites like Kodak Gallery, Shutterfly, Flickr, Photobucket, and others, where the bride, her family, guests, and the rest of the bridal party can order the ones they want on the cheap.

"My sister was able to borrow a Polaroid camera from one of her friends, and we used that for everyone to fill the guest book with fun shots they took right then!" says one resourceful bridesmaid from San Diego.

Here are your budget-saving strategies when it comes to photos and video:

• Get free accounts at the top online photo-sharing sites, so that you can keep an eye on their weekly sales. As I write this, I just received an email from KodakGallery.com about their five-day ten-cent prints sale. Sold! I have images from a party that have been waiting months for the best print-out deal.

• Look for free shipping offers at online photo developing sites, and put that code to good use. You'd be shocked at how many people pass up a free shipping offer because they forget to plug in that code. And see if you can use the site's coupon code *plus* extra savings coupon codes you find on your favorite coupon websites and through searches for double or triple the savings. Many sites accept more than one coupon per order!

• Comparison shop for the per-print fees at insta-development kiosks seen in CVS, Walgreens, and other stores, and then compare them to the per-print prices at your local Costco or Sam's Club. It might not seem like a few cents here and there would make a difference, but when you have tons of photos you want to print, it does add up!

• Eliminate shipping by using developing sites like KodakGallery.com that allow you to pick up your prints at CVS or other stores.

• Use your own home computer photo editing software to crop, color-fix, and even *slenderize* your photos. Then, rather than spending a fortune on your own ink, it's often smarter to save your edited images, and get them printed at a ten-cent per print site.

Stop Right There!

Don't use the office computers and printers to print out your photos, as we saw suggested on one bridal message board. That's just going to get you fired if you get caught. Shame on that poster for suggesting theft!

• Get acquainted with some of the fun photo-art sites online. Picnik .com is one of the most popular photo-editing sites with a quality free level, allowing you to remove red-eyes, crop, and use fonts to personalize your images. They also have several premium levels that open up additional tools, including a very interesting Clone Tool that allows you to *add or remove* things from your images. So if you want to erase the bride's mean, scowling future mother-in-law from a group shot, you can!

• If you live an eco-conscious lifestyle, sharing images online is going to make you happy, as well as save you money, and for those pictures you do wish to print out, you can take your image card to a print shop that uses green printing practices like soy ink.

Save Money Later!

Photos from these get-togethers make great photos for your friends' birthdays and holiday gifts, too! So rather than spend $50 on an impressive gift card for a friend's present, you can upload one of your fun duo photos—maybe one from the shower, or from the wedding's after-party—to an inexpensive photo developing site for huge savings and a fun, personalized gift for her, under $10 in many cases. Often with free shipping.

• As for frames, you'll find plenty for under $5 each at your local craft shop. Sign on to that craft shop's member email lists to receive special coupons in the mail or online, and get an additional 20 percent off of *that* price, too.

• Bartering can get you a friend's expertise with video editing! If your friend has top-notch video editing software—and knows how to use it!—perhaps he or she can edit your wedding season videos into one fun presentation for the bride in exchange for a few trays of your homemade lasagna or your help with painting her new home's kitchen.

CHAPTER 16

Alterations

*I*n order for your dress or gown to look perfect on you, to hang just right, and to show off your best assets, alterations are *essential*. Yes, you could buy a dress off the rack at a department store and have it look just fine on you, but even Stacy and Clinton on TLC's *What Not to Wear* are constantly recommending the instant fixes that only a talented seamstress or tailor can do. With just the taking-up of your straps by an inch or two, your shape looks entirely different (and far better) than if your dress were allowed to hang as low as the straps allow. And a tailored fit at your waist can make you look slimmer.

If you're going to invest in the dress, invest in making it look its best.

If you're among the bridesmaids who found and bought their dresses through a bridal shop, your alterations might be free. This is one of the services often provided at the most chic boutiques . . . but keep in mind that the dress itself *could* cost a bit more than you might find elsewhere. You always have to look at the give-and-take, configure the perks, and see if that $200 dress is a steal when it also includes $75-worth of free alterations. "My dress was such a challenge, owing to my small chest and big hips, that I knew I was in for it with a seamstress's charges," says one bridesmaid from Los Angeles. "So when we found out that alterations were included in the price, we all voted to get the salon dress rather than the department store dresses that cost $30 less."

Here's how to arrange great alterations on a budget:

WHO'S GOING TO DO IT?

It takes a great seamstress or tailor to create a great result. A talented pro can take one look at you and one look at the dress, and know just how to work magic with seams, tucks, and hems. So invest extra time in finding the best expert you can.

You Can Do Better

According to TheWeddingReport.com's survey, the average amount spent by bridesmaids on their alterations in 2009 was $56.

• Ask the bride who she's using to work on her gown. Ask recently married friends if they worked with an independent seamstress they found outside of their gown shop. *Ask professionals in the wedding industry—such as florists and wedding coordinators—who they know in the business, since it's a small world, and all the experts know one another.* Those who have comparison-shopped can tell you who is priced best.

• Don't just go to your regular dry cleaner's alterations worker. Yes, you may know they do good work. But the average dry cleaner alterations expert has more experience with pant hems than with complicated seams in satin material, boning in corset tops, and other challenges. This pro might not be the best option for you, even if the price is pleasing.

• Check out traditional, non-bridal tailors. I found a fabulous one in my hometown who I hired to tailor my bridesmaid's dress for my brother's wedding. His price was *half* what my dress cleaner's tailoring staff charged, and he did an amazing job in just a few days.

• See if it's free from the store! Many department stores and boutiques have their own alterations experts on-staff, and sometimes the store offers basic alterations for *free* when you buy the dress. Ask lots of questions about what's free and what's extra, and if the alterations pro offers a free initial consultation.

Look for an Alterations Specialist, a talented pro who has years of experience working on all types of attire, from basic businesswear to the most complicated couture dresses. Visit the shop, meet with the expert, ask to see the price sheet, and bring the dress along to see just what might be involved, and at what cost.

Don't Make This Huge Mistake!

I've seen suggestions on bridal message boards telling brides and bridesmaids to have a friend do their tailoring, and unless your friend is a seamstress by vocation, this can often be a *bad* idea. When a well-meaning friend with a sewing machine agrees to take up your straps or do your hem, she might not be aware that your chiffon or silky fabric is going to be hugely challenging. We've all seen contestants on *Project Runway* wind up with puckery seams due to a satiny fabric's slippery texture, and if *they* can't get it right, how can an untrained friend? It's not a savings of money if your gown looks like a fifth-grade sewing class worked on it. For an hour. So this is one of those areas where it's best to invest in expert tailoring work.

WHAT TO KNOW

• A great tailor can add straps to the strapless dress that the rest of the bridesmaids have chosen, for under $10.

• Remember, details on your dress can make alterations a bit pricier. A beaded bodice will present more of a challenge to your tailor, since he or she might have to painstakingly remove some of the hand-sewn baubles to get that seam altered . . . then hand-sew those beads back on in a pattern to match the original. Time equals money, so your gown's embellishments can add a chunk of change to your expense.

• Ask if the tailor charges a flat fee, stated up front, or if the charge is going to be by-the-hour, or per-task. If your dress needs just some simple hemming and strapwork, the flat fee might be best. That challenging bead-works could take *hours*, which is quite a gamble financially.

• Ask if the seamstress works with your gown's specific type of fabric. Some experts say that they hate working with certain types of fabrics—like those slippery or chiffon-y fabrics, or lacy, beaded fabrics—so they may charge more for their time and aggravation.

What Were Those Expensive-to-Alter Fabrics, Again?

You read about these in the dress chapter, and here they are as your reminder. The fabrics that often cost way more to alter are:

• Chiffon

• Organza

• Satin

• Silk

• Intricately beaded fabrics and laces

• Wear your wedding-day undergarments—just like the bride does—so that the seamstress can fit your dress to the uplift of that great bra you're going to wear that day, or adjust seams to work with the effects of the body slimmer you'll have on. And wear your wedding day shoes, as well, so the seamstress can hem to the right height.

• Don't go for fittings too far in advance of the wedding, or else your body size might be a bit different when the wedding day arrives. Going too early could mean that you'll have to go *again* later, doubling your expenses, to refit the dress to your smaller or larger body shape. Ask your seamstress candidate to recommend the best timing for your initial visit and subsequent fittings. A month is usually enough time prior to the wedding for your alterations, for many experts. *And some will charge you a rush fee at the one-month mark.* For the best results in the best timing at the best price, customize your tailoring schedule with the pro you've found to be best.

• Sign on for just one or two fittings, not the four or five the bride will need to alter her dress.

Fabulous Saves and Solutions

A top-quality fabric tape, again, is going to be a fabulous, inexpensive Save for your straps or to keep a wrap top from revealing too much cleavage. So buy a few packs, because you're going to fall in love with this product, if you aren't already a devoted fan.

Uh-Oh . . .

What happens if you've gained weight since you ordered the dress?

It might seem like your only option is to order another dress in the next size up. That *could* be a solution if you ordered your dress from a department store or a shop like Ann Taylor, where formal and bridesmaid dresses are still available online and are easy to return and exchange for the next bigger size. You might only have to pay $4 or so for return shipping. If this is the case, problem solved for not a lot of cash.

If, though, the dress was found on sale at one of these stores or online, it might not be available anymore.

You can have a talented tailor give your dress a seamless alteration to give you more room with a panel added to the side or back, or—as I had done with one of my own bridesmaid dresses after I gained ten pounds before a wedding—have that tailor create a *corset-laced back*. My amazing tailor saw that I couldn't get my zipper up the top four inches, so he designed a pretty lace-up effect with perfectly sewn circular holes on either side of a V-cut in the back, plus a braided length of cord that laced up the back and tied beautifully. And it cost me $30. Including the cord. Way less than the rush fees would have been for me to order a larger dress ... which would have been so depressing! I got the alteration, my dress was saved, and it didn't wipe out my budget.

Ask your tailor or seamstress to show you photos of the kinds of dress rescues they've done. Great pros have Before and After photos to share, and it's amazing what a talented expert can do.

CHAPTER 17

Other Surprise Expenses

*O*f course, some unexpected, additional expenses will pop up during the course of your season as a bridesmaid. In most cases, it's $20 here, $30 there ... harmless amounts that aren't worth worrying about during those first few months when every time you whip out your cash or credit card, *it's so worth it*. But then ... a few months later, you hear yourself levying that audible *sigh* when you have to shell out yet again.

For some bridesmaids, these Extras can add up to hundreds of dollars ... maybe even grand-totalling to more than the cost of the dress! *And* the shoes!

So in this chapter, we're going to look at some smart money-saving strategies for the most common "budget-suckers" out there:

1. Bridal show admission: If the bride invites you to attend a bridal show with her, be aware that not all shows have free admission. Check your regional bridal website, or Google the name of the show and the word *coupon* to get a freebie pass. Wedding coordinators also often have free passes to give out, so the bride might want to make a call.

2. Luncheons: Wanting to share great quality time with her bridesmaids, the bride might plan regular luncheons or dinners so that everyone can get together, go over the next wave of plans and details, have a few

cocktails, and just hang out. That's *fabulous*, since it's important to keep your close connection with the bride and get to know your co-planning bridesmaid sisters better, so that you're all more comfortable working together along the way. The problem is when the bride—or even the maid of honor, who prefers in-person planning meetings for the bridal shower and bachelorette party—plans get-togethers a little too often . . . and with each one set for a different restaurant, the bill-splitting adds up. Yes, it would be considered good etiquette for the bride to pick up the entire bill for the planning lunch she's invited you to, but that doesn't always turn out to be the case. Here are some ways to cut costs on these gatherings:

• Going to lunch at a family-style restaurant that offers a special 2-for-$10 lunch special, including an appetizer. At the time of this writing, Applebees and Chili's were among the restaurant chains in my area who offered this fabulous, price-cutting plan for lunches.

• Going to lunch, not dinner, which can save half the cost.

• Arrange with the bridesmaids that each of you will take turns hosting an informal cocktail party on a weekday or weekend night, with the menu consisting of hummus and pita chips, fresh fruit, veggie dips, all-natural whole-grain chips, and other healthy snacks. You pull out those bottles of wine you've received as gifts over the past few months, plus a fruity punch or sangria. When you host once for $30 total, it saves you a bundle.

• Agree as a group to go for coffee instead, which gives you the option of just getting a chai tea and skipping the lemon scone or fat-infused chocolate muffin.

3. Permits: Check to see if the neighborhood association where your shower will take place requires a permit for gatherings and parking, and do the same with the park service if your party will take place at a gazebo or will feature outdoor cooking at a nearby park area. Spending $20 on a permit with smart advance thinking will save you *hundreds* in tickets that can surprise you when the authorities approach your outdoor party. And of course, you have to get a permit if your event on any public or park grounds will include serving alcohol. So if you think a coed shower at the park, with a cookout at the gazebo and a softball tournament, is a great idea, there are

about six permits you have to get. Including one to use the softball field. I wish I was kidding, but these are the days we live in, and townships have to make a buck.

Permit Research

When you call the township or park service to inquire about permits, make sure you talk to a real, live person—and get that person's name—rather than just go by the information you find on the township's website or . . . *please don't do this!* . . . on a bridal website where some random bride wrote about the steps she took to get permits. Laws and rules change all the time, so it's ultra-smart to talk to or meet with the actual person in charge of granting and arranging permits for any gatherings.

4. Insurance: Spending a little extra on insurance is *always* a good idea when you're shipping gowns to the other bridesmaids or having your gown shipped to you. With so many parcels in the air and on the ground with the postal service, UPS, and FedEx at any one time, it's easy for a box to get waylaid. And if it's *your* dress that disappears, you have a pricey reordering and rush fee on your hands. So always spend the few bucks it takes to insure important shipments. On a completely different insurance topic, any at-home party such as a bridal shower introduces so many dangers . . . especially in this litigious society. If a guest trips and falls on an outdoor garden pathway and breaks her ankle, guess who she's going to sue? The owner of the house. If it's snowy outside and a guest slips on your icy walkway, hits her head, and gets a concussion, her doctor bills are on you. So talk to your insurance expert about getting an inexpensive additional rider on your home insurance to protect you from situations like this. It doesn't cost a lot, but it can save you thousands of dollars if anything unexpected happens. Brides and grooms are adding extra

insurance policies to their plans if they're having an at-home wedding or pre-wedding parties, so it's a great idea to add this expense to your bridesmaid budget. Again, a small amount in costs for a rider versus tons of money in doctor's bills *plus the pain and suffering that some guests claim* . . . there's just no question here. Look into it.

5. Cleanup: Set aside an extra $100 to $150 in your bridesmaid group's emergency fund in case you need to pay for any professional cleaning service to remove red wine stains from the rug at the bride's mother's house, or to replace any broken rented wineglasses or plates. Whatever's left unused from this fund gets refunded to all the bridesmaids.

6. Tipping: Set aside a healthy amount for tips, so that you can reward any servers or delivery people, or your beauty experts, for their great work.

Part Four

Troubleshooting

CHAPTER 18

The 10 Biggest Bridesmaid Budget Mistakes

*L*earn from the mistakes of those bridesmaids who came before you, avoiding the kinds of huge money-wasters *they* experienced when they gave in to some very common pressures. Some of these bridesmaids overspent by fifty dollars and some saw *hundreds* of dollars float away. Some dug themselves into stressful debts, had to cancel their own planned vacations, and all wound up very, very mad at themselves.

You won't wind up broke and angry, though. You get to save yourself from these money land mines. Just keep these ten biggest budget mistakes in mind:

1. Letting the Louder Bridesmaid Rule. Find a way to say no to the pushy, controlling bridesmaid who wants to add extra plans and prices.

2. Not Offering Non-Money Alternatives. Sign on to several DIY projects and support roles (such as gathering addresses for shower guests, or working setup and cleanup) and save over $200.

3. Trying to Be Nice (and Fit In). Don't say yes to new ideas and bigger expenses just to be liked and be the new friend in their circle.

4. Not Acting Early Enough. Speak up right away to let everyone know you have this book and great ways to save them all lots of money. Stall, and they'll start setting pricey plans in action.

5. Not Admitting You're on a Budget. Put your pride away. *Everyone* is on a budget, and there's no shame in it anymore. And when you speak up to the bride, the maid of honor, and the bridesmaids about being on a budget, you allow all the other on-a-budget bridesmaids to speak freely of their money crunches, as well, which gets you all on the same budget-planning page.

6. Not Establishing Your Own Emergency Fund. Make sure you have enough money to cover your own bills and allow you enough of your own spending money, so that bridesmaid expenses don't wipe you out and hurt your roommate or spouse.

7. Counting on "Maybe Money." Your tax refund. Birthday money. A payback from a friend to whom you lent money months ago, and she's promised to pay you back next week. Never spend money—or *promise* to spend money—you *expect* to have someday soon . . . because it might not arrive. And then you'll be locked into an expensive dress or party plans you originally agreed to but cannot afford.

8. Not Being Organized. If you lose the receipt from the dress shop, you won't be able to prove you paid cash for the deposit on the day you bought your dress. Yes, online banking and credit card statements will show you proof of purchase when a dress shop claims you never paid up, but if you

used a debit card as many people do to avoid credit card debt, you need that print receipt as your proof . . . and as the only thing that's going to prevent that shady shop from demanding you pay again. Keep organized files of your receipts to keep from missing deadlines, angering the bride and the group, and costing you late fees. And keep all emails regarding the wedding in one folder on your email system, since some systems automatically wipe out your Inbox and Sent messages that are more than three months old.

9. Not Being a Smart Consumer. Shopping from an unsecure site, or buying from a shady vendor on an auction site, is a quick way not only to waste money but to have your identity stolen . . . which is *really* expensive. You know the smart shopping rules of Internet purchases, so stick with them and save.

10. Buying a Dress You *Hope* to Fit Into. If you don't get into that 6, you'll have to buy a new dress or pay for a seamstress or tailor to add an extra panel or let out your seams. And that feels *awful*. Order a dress in the size you are now, maybe even one size larger, and enjoy the easy and inexpensive tailoring sessions that make you feel fabulous and don't require extra charges such as postage and rush fees.

CHAPTER 19

Money Clashes with Others

could give you every half-priced, super-discount website in the world to help you land spectacular budget bridesmaid purchases, but you'll need a few extra tips to save you money (and frustration) when it comes to working with other bridesmaids who may not share your same need to cut costs. Here are some solutions for you:

• If the maid of honor and bridesmaids are emailing links to super-expensive dresses, don't worry about emailing back with a friendly message of, "These are a bit above my budget level. How about these?" and attach links to the fabulous, budget-friendly dresses you've found. It won't solve anything if you're simply saying no to what they send. You'll get far better success when you send images.

• If the bridesmaids are notorious fashionistas likely to select designer dresses, call the bride now to see if she's decided to let everyone choose their own gown styles. You might just nudge her into allowing it.

• If you're in charge of collecting money for a particular part of the shower plans or other task and some of the other bridesmaids haven't yet sent you their checks, email them directly to say, "The order can't go in until everyone sends their checks, and the rush fee for an order placed after (date) is going to cost everyone an extra $40 apiece. So please do send your

207

check to me at (address) by next Friday at the latest." Send this email with a confirm receipt request for when it's viewed.

• If you're in charge of an order, set the Payment Due By date at least two weeks before the actual deadline to leave time for stragglers to get their payments to you.

• If the others forget to send you shipping payments, just email with a reminder that an extra $5 is due. And end with a cheery advance thank-you for their payment.

• Don't send "pay up" emails when you're angry or frustrated, since your terse tone will likely come through. Always make sure that your emailed messages contain positive language and even a smiley face, so that no one misinterprets your reminder email as a bossy affront.

• Practice good leadership and send each bridesmaid a thank-you email when you receive their payments.

WHEN IT'S THE BRIDE

The bride has big wishes and dreams for her wedding day, and some of those wishes and dreams spill over into your portion of the plans. Some brides see this as their time to shine, to be in control, to have people *finally* listen to *them*. While this is a minority of brides, you might be stuck with one.

If the bride is among the *very* rare ones who pick the dress for the bridesmaids, saying, "This is what it's going to be," you're in for a rough ride. Some bridesmaids drop out of the bridal party at this point. And some, realizing that this is how the bride is and has always been, just shift their budget around to make room for the $300 dress the bride wants them to wear. They'll find ways to save elsewhere, in something the bride has no control over.

What are you going to do? That's the sigh of the bridesmaid who happens to be stuck with a steamroller bride, and it's a fact that some expenses will be prescribed to you with no negotiations possible.

Hey, you agreed to be my bridesmaid! is the battle cry of the bride who doesn't enjoy hearing complaints or requests from anyone, pulled as she is from all sides by her mother who wants some things her way and her future mother-in-law who also wants to change some things the bride wants. The poor bride is under a ton of pressure, and when her bridesmaids start approaching with objections, the bridesmaids are the safe ones to unload upon. Sad, but true. The bride can't very well unleash on her future mother-in-law, nor on her mother, who may be paying for the wedding. So even if all you're asking for is a change to the style of strap, you might get your head bitten off. And chewed. And spat back at you.

Don't Hurt the Bride

Here's one huge warning when it comes to approaching a Money Clash with the bride: Never go to her and say that all the bridesmaids want a change to her plan. Because all she'll hear is that the bridesmaids talked about her behind her back, hate her idea, and you drew the short straw in having to tell her. Instead, tread lightly. Focus on the solution. Suggest that she give you a few days to find some additional options that she might like even more, at an even better price. Promise to show them to her first, and then she can pick the ones that are shown to the bridesmaids. She gets to be in control. She's respected as the In-Charge One, and you get your less expensive possibilities on the table.

There's only so much you can do to get the bride to swing her wishes toward what you can best afford. The best relationships are formed with compromise and mutual respect, and the best friendships are ones in which you would do anything to *find a way* to make your friend happy, without hurting yourself. The bride doesn't want you destroyed financially. She has your best interests in mind. All it takes to avoid Money Clashes with her is honesty, communication, a sense of humor, and offering up your assurance that everything is going to be fabulous for her.

And remember this: You didn't talk only about money with the bride before the wedding, so don't do that now. Keep the many playful, fun, and indulgent dimensions of your relationship going with girls' nights out, movie night at your place, phone calls to share a funny story, and listening to her talk about anything . . . wedding-related or not. The priceless thing to the bride is having a great friend she can be herself with now. And that's just the kind of friend you are.

CHAPTER 20

If You Have to Step Out of the Bridal Party

*T*his chapter is not going to touch on whether or not you *should* step out of the bridal party, or on any of the details surrounding why you decided or agreed to exit the bridesmaid lineup, drama-free or not. We're just going to stick to the money issue . . . namely, how to recoup what you've already invested, what you may not be likely to get back, and how to be okay with that.

Stepping out of a bridal party might happen early in the process, or it might have to happen just a few months before the big day. You might have spent a little, or a lot. And now with your bridesmaid title gone from you, your question remains: *Can I get any of my money back?*

The bottom line is this: If you've already given money toward the bridal shower or bachelorette party, it's considered a big Etiquette Don't to try to get that money back. After all, the group of bridesmaids divided the expenses, and it would open a huge can of worms if you now injured their budgets with the requirement that they now hand over more money to cover your share. Instead, your money is already spent, and your name stays on the hosts' names list even if you're not a bridesmaid anymore and even if you're not even going to be *at* the bridal shower anymore.

The same applies for your share that you might already have paid for the bachelorette party. Your name stays on as host, and that's your contribution

211

to the bride's big celebration. It's quite common for non-bridesmaids to be hosts of this party, so you're okay in the precedent department.

Any money you spent is already spent, and with the parties portion of a bridesmaid's role, it's very rare for a new, replacement bridesmaid to step in, refund you your share, and then have life go on smoothly. So don't waste your energy and stress everyone out by looking for that solution, that refund. Everyone has too much to do. Just remind yourself that you spent the shower and other celebration money to give the bride a fabulous time, and that's still important no matter what your status is.

The one area where you can most often recoup your investment is with the bridesmaid gown. Depending on the timing of your exit from the bridal party, you may have the ability to return it or trade it in as your solution. Here's how:

• If you bought from a bridal salon that has a return policy (most don't!), check your purchase order and receipt to find out what percentage of your money you can get back. If you ordered the dress and it has not come in yet, you may be able to cancel your order and get a full refund, depending upon when you request your refund. Or, the contract and purchase order may have a stated time frame saying that only half of your deposit will be refunded after thirty days, for instance. And some shops will pull an amount of money out as a nonrefundable fee to cover their time and efforts in putting a stop to your order.

• If you ordered or purchased your dress from a department store or clothing store, you're very likely to get a full refund minus your original shipping costs when you follow their returns procedures and policies. (This is why it's smart to have a file folder or box in which you'll keep receipts, and also keep tags on any clothing purchases until the last minute!)

• If you ordered or purchased your dress from a department store or clothing store, and it's now more than thirty days since you bought the dress, contact their customer service department to see how returns are handled. Some stores will refund your credit card, and some will give you a store credit gift card instead.

• *If* it's early enough in the process and other bridesmaids have not ordered their dresses yet, perhaps one of them would like to pay you for your ordered-early dress, which you might have nabbed during a limited-time sale for 30 percent off! The maid of honor may be able to help you arrange this.

• *If* the dress is wear-again-able, just keep it and wear it to another event, saving yourself the need to buy a new formal or cocktail party dress in the future, which might cost 10 to 20 percent more down the road.

No matter what the timing, no matter what the circumstances, you need to decide what's worth fighting for when it comes to the return of your money. Only you can decide the value of the time and conflict that might be lost to a battle, as well as the cost to your relationships. So weigh your situation before you fire off any type of pay-me-back email.

Appendices

Contacts

Name: _____
Cell: _____
Phone: _____
E-mail: _____

Name: _____
Cell: _____
Phone: _____
E-mail: _____

Name: _____
Cell: _____
Phone: _____
E-mail: _____

Name: _____
Cell: _____
Phone: _____
E-mail: _____

Name: _____
Cell: _____
Phone: _____
E-mail: _____

Name: _____
Cell: _____
Phone: _____
E-mail: _____

Name: _____

Cell: _____

Phone: _____

E-mail: _____

Name: _____

Cell: _____

Phone: _____

E-mail: _____

Name: _____

Cell: _____

Phone: _____

E-mail: _____

Name: _____

Cell: _____

Phone: _____

E-mail: _____

Name: _____

Cell: _____

Phone: _____

E-mail: _____

Name: _____

Cell: _____

Phone: _____

E-mail: _____

Deadlines

Keep track of all of your Bridesmaid Delivery Deadlines right here!

ITEM OR TASK (SHOPPING, DIY, CALL TO BE MADE)	FINAL DECISION TO BE MADE	DETAILS, SIZES, COLORS COLLECTED	DEPOSIT DUE	FINAL PAYMENT DUE, TASK COMPLETED OR PICKED UP

ITEM OR TASK (SHOPPING, DIY, CALL TO BE MADE)	FINAL DECISION TO BE MADE	DETAILS, SIZES, COLORS COLLECTED	DEPOSIT DUE	FINAL PAYMENT DUE, TASK COMPLETED OR PICKED UP

DEADLINES

219

Payment Ledger

ITEM OR SERVICE	DEPOSIT DUE DATE	DEPOSIT PAID ✓	FINAL AMOUNT DUE DATE	FINAL PAID ✓

ITEM OR SERVICE	DEPOSIT DUE DATE	DEPOSIT PAID ✓	FINAL AMOUNT DUE DATE	FINAL PAID ✓

PAYMENT LEDGER

221

Shopping Lists

- [ ] _____
- [ ] _____
- [ ] _____
- [ ] _____
- [ ] _____
- [ ] _____
- [ ] _____
- [ ] _____
- [ ] _____
- [ ] _____
- [ ] _____
- [ ] _____
- [ ] _____
- [ ] _____
- [ ] _____
- [ ] _____
- [ ] _____
- [ ] _____
- [ ] _____
- [ ] _____
- [ ] _____
- [ ] _____
- [ ] _____
- [ ] _____

- [ ] _____
- [ ] _____
- [ ] _____
- [ ] _____
- [ ] _____
- [ ] _____
- [ ] _____
- [ ] _____
- [ ] _____
- [ ] _____
- [ ] _____
- [ ] _____
- [ ] _____
- [ ] _____
- [ ] _____
- [ ] _____
- [ ] _____
- [ ] _____
- [ ] _____
- [ ] _____
- [ ] _____
- [ ] _____
- [ ] _____
- [ ] _____
- [ ] _____
- [ ] _____
- [ ] _____

Favorite Stores and Sources

Gowns

STORE NAME	WEBSITE	CONTACT INFO

Shoes

STORE NAME	WEBSITE	CONTACT INFO

Accessories

STORE NAME	WEBSITE	CONTACT INFO

Beauty and Spa

SALON NAME	WEBSITE	CONTACT INFO

Bridal Shower Needs

STORE NAME	WEBSITE	CONTACT INFO

DIY and Craft Needs

STORE NAME	WEBSITE	CONTACT INFO

Other

STORE NAME	WEBSITE	CONTACT INFO

Favorite Websites for *My Future Wedding*

WEBSITE NAME	URL

Plan B List

Dress: _____
_____

Shoes: _____
_____

Accessories: _____
_____

Alterations: _____
_____

Beauty Plan: _____
_____

Shower Location: _____
_____

Shower Theme: _____
_____

Shower Invitations: _____
_____

Shower Décor: _____
_____

Shower Menu: _____
_____

Shower Drinks: _____
_____

Shower Cake: _____
_____

Shower Desserts: _____
_____

Shower Gift: _____
_____

Shower Games: _____
_____

Lodging: _____
_____

Group Wedding Gift: _____
_____

Other: _____
_____

Ideas for My Wedding/Special Celebrations

Resources

This list is purely for your research use, and does not imply endorsement or recommendation of the companies or products. Since websites change over the course of time, we apologize if any Web addresses have changed since the time of this printing.

BRIDESMAID'S GOWN

Bridal Sources

- After Six: www.aftersix.com
- Aimee Monet: www.weddingchannel.com
- Alfred Angelo: www.alfredangelo.com
- Alvina Valenta: www.jlmcouture.com
- Ann Taylor Weddings and Events: www.anntaylor.com
- Aria: www.ariadress.com
- Bari Jay Bridesmaids: www.barijay.com
- Bill Levkoff: www.billlevkoff.com
- Bridesmaids.com: www.bridesmaids.com
- Chadwick's: www.chadwicks.com
- Champagne Formals: www.champagneformals.com
- David's Bridal: www.davidsbridal.com
- Dessy Creations: www.dessy.com
- Eden Maids: www.edenbridals.com
- Group USA: www.groupusa.com
- Impressions Bridesmaids: www.impressionsbridal.com
- JC Penney Bridal Shop: www.jcpenney.com
- J. Crew Weddings: www.jcrew.com
- Jessica McClintock: www.jessicamcclintock.com
- Jim Hjelm Occasions: www.jimhjelmoccasions.com
- Jordan: www.jordanfashions.com
- Melissa Sweet Bridal: www.melissasweet.com

- Moonlight Me Too! Bridesmaids: www.moonlightbridal.com
- Mon Cheri Bridals: www.mcbridals.com
- Mori Lee: www.morileeinc.com
- Net Bride: www.netbride.com
- Rhyme: www.rhymecouture.com
- Saison Blanche: www.saisonblanche.com
- Sarah Danielle Evenings: www.sinceritybridal.com
- Spiegel: www.spiegel.com
- Vera Wang Maids Collection: www.verawang.com
- Vineyard Collection: www.priscillaofboston.com
- Vivian Bridal: www.vivianbridal.com
- Watters and Watters: www.watters.com

Department Stores
- Bloomingdales: www.bloomingdales.com
- JC Penney: www.jcpenney.com
- Lord & Taylor: www.lordandtaylor.com
- Macy's: www.macys.com
- Nordstrom: www.nordstrom.com

Outlet Stores and Others
- Outlet Bound: www.outletbound.com
- The Find: www.thefind.com

SHOES AND ACCESSORIES

Please revisit the bridesmaid dress designers' websites above to find lovely shoes and trunk sales for shoes and accessories!

- Aldo Shoes: www.aldoshoes.com
- Ann Taylor: www.anntaylor.com
- Bare Essentials: www.bareessentials.com
- Bridal Shoes: www.bridalshoes.com
- David's Bridal: www.davidsbridal.com

- Discount Wedding Shoes: www.discountweddingshoes.com
- DSW: www.dsw.com
- Dyeables: www.dyeables.com
- Dyeable Shoes Online: www.dyeableshoesonline.com
- Dyeable Shoe Store: www.dyeableshoestore.com
- Factory Brand Shoes: www.factorybrandshoes.com
- Fenaroli for Regalia: www.fenaroli.com
- JC Penney: www.jcpenney.com
- Kenneth Cole: www.kennethcole.com
- Kohls: www.kohls.com
- Laura Lee Designs: www.lauraleedesigns.com
- Love My Shoes: www.lovemyshoes.com
- Macy's: www.macys.com
- Masseys: www.masseys.com
- MJM Shoes: www.mjmdesignershoes.com
- My Little Pretty: www.mylittlepretty.com
- MyShoes.com: www.myshoes.com
- Nina Footwear: www.ninashoes.com
- Nordstrom's: www.nordstroms.com
- Salon Shoes: www.salonshoes.com
- Shoe Buy: www.shoebuy.com
- Shoes.com: www.shoes.com
- Shoes Direct: www.shoesdirect.com
- Shoes To Match: www.shoestomatch.com
- Spanx: www.spanx.com
- Steve Madden: www.stevemadden.com
- Target: www.target.com
- Victoria's Secret: www.victoriassecret.com
- Wanted Shoes: www.wantedshoes.com
- Watters and Watters: www.watters.com
- Zappos: www.zappos.com

BEAUTY

- Avon: www.avon.com
- Beauty on Call: www.beautyoncall.com
- Bobbi Brown Essentials: www.bobbibrown.com
- Care Fair: www.carefair.com
- Clinique: www.clinique.com
- Elizabeth Arden: www.elizabetharden.com
- Estee Lauder: www.esteelauder.com
- Eve: www.eve.com
- Fresh Look (contact lenses): www.freshlook.com
- iBeauty: www.ibeauty.com
- Lancome: www.lancome.com
- L'Oreal: www.loreal.com
- Mac: www.maccosmetics.com
- Makeover Studio: www.makeoverstudio.com (choose your face shape and experiment with makeup shades and looks)
- Max Factor: www.maxfactor.com
- Maybelline: www.maybelline.com
- Neutrogena: www.neutrogena.com
- Pantene: www.pantene.com
- Reflect.com (customized beauty products): www.reflect.com
- Rembrandt: www.rembrandt.com
- Revlon: www.revlon.com
- Sephora: www.sephora.com

INVITATIONS

- An Invitation to Buy Nationwide: www.invitations4sale.com
- Anna Griffin Invitation Design: www.annagriffin.com
- Birchcraft: www.birchcraft.com
- Botanical PaperWorks: www.botanicalpaperworks.com
- Crane and Company: www.crane.com
- Invite Site (made from recycled paper): www.invitesite.com

- MountainCow: www.mountaincow.com
- Now and Forever: www.now-and-forever.com
- PaperStyle.com: www.paperstyle.com
- Papyrus: www.papyrusonline.com
- Precious Collection: www.preciouscollection.com
- PSA Essentials: www.psaessentials.com
- Vismara Invitations: www.vismarainvitations.com
- You're Invited: www.youreinvited.com

Online Invitations
- Evite: www.evite.com
- Hallmark: www.hallmark.com
- Blue Mountain Arts: www.bluemountain.com

Postage Stamps
- Mountaincow: www.mountaincow.com
- Personal Stamps: www.personalstamps.com
- United States Postal Service: www.usps.gov

CRAFTS AND PAPER
- A.C. Moore: www.acmoore.com
- Flax Art: www.flaxart.com
- Hobby Lobby: www.hobbylobby.com
- Michaels: www.michaels.com
- Mountaincow: www.mountaincow.com
- My Wedding Labels: www.myweddinglabels.com
- Office Max: www.officemax.com
- Paper Access: www.paperaccess.com
- Paper Direct: www.paperdirect.com
- Scrapjazz: www.scrapjazz.com
- Staples: www.staples.com

PHOTO DEVELOPING AND ALBUMS

- Adesso Albums: www.adessoalbums.com
- Exposures: www.exposuresonline.com
- Flickr: www.flickr.com
- Fuji: www.fujifilm.com
- Kodak Gallery: www.kodakgallery.com
- Photo Bucket: www.photobucket.com
- Shutterfly: www.shutterfly.com

LINENS

- BBJ Linen: www.bbjlinen.com
- Chair Covers Online: www.chaircoversonline.com
- Source One: www.sourceone.com

RENTALS

- American Rental Association: www.ararental.org
- Association of Bridal Consultants: www.bridalassn.com
- International Special Event Society: www.ises.org

FLOWERS AND GREENERY IDEAS

- Better Homes and Gardens: www.bhg.com
- HGTV: www.hgtv.com
- P. Allen Smith: www.pallensmith.com
- Romantic Flowers: www.romanticflowers.com
- Sierra Flower Finder: www.sierraflowerfinder.com

FAVORS

- Godiva: www.godiva.com
- Charming Favours: www.charmingfavours.com
- Bath & Body Works: www.bathandbodyworks.com
- Beau-Coup: www.beau-coup.com

- Bella Terra: www.bellaterra.net
- Bliss Weddings Market: www.blissweddingsmarket.com
- Cheryl&Co (cookies, brownies, amazing sweets): www.cherylandco.com
- Illuminations: www.illuminations.com
- Kate Aspen: www.kateaspen.com
- M&M's: www.mms.com
- Moma Store: www.momastore.org
- My Wedding Labels: www.myweddinglabels.com
- Pearl River (Asian-themed favors): www.pearlriver.com
- Pier 1: www.pier1.com
- Wedding Things: www.weddingthings.com

Favor Packaging
- Bayley's Boxes: www.bayleysboxes.com
- Michael's Crafts: www.michaels.com

FOOD, RECIPES, AND MENU ITEMS
- Ben & Jerry's: www.benjerry.com
- Better Homes & Gardens: www.bhg.com
- Food Network: www.foodtv.com
- Gail Watson: www.gailwatsoncakes.com
- Martha Stewart: www.marthastewart.com
- Mixing Bowl: www.mixingbowl.com
- The Food Network: www.foodtv.com

Cakes and Desserts
- Cheryl&Co: www.cherylandco.com
- Martha Stewart: www.marthastewart.com
- Mixing Bowl: www.mixingbowl.com
- Ron Ben-Israel Wedding Cakes: www.weddingcakes.com
- Wilton's (cake and cupcake supplies): www.wiltons.com

Drinks

- Better Homes & Gardens: www.bhg.com
- Drink Gus: www.drinkgus.com
- Fizzy Lizzy: www.fizzylizzy.com
- Food Network: www.foodtv.com
- Steazsoda: www.steazsoda.com

Wine and Champagne

- Food and Wine Magazine: www.foodandwine.com
- Wine.com: www.wine.com
- Wine Searcher: www.winesearcher.com
- Wine Spectator: www.winespectator.com

Caterers and Chefs

- International Association of Culinary Professionals: www.iacp.com
- International Special Events Society: www.ises.com
- National Association of Catering Executives: www.nace.net
- Personal Chef Association: www.personalchef.com

WAREHOUSE STORES

- BJ's Wholesale Club: www.bjs.com
- Costco: www.costco.com
- Sam's Club: www.samsclub.com

TRAVEL

Price Comparison and Booking Sites

- AAA: www.aaa.com
- Airfare Watchdog: www.airfarewatchdog.com
- Expedia: www.expedia.com
- Farecast: www.farecast.com
- Fare Compare: www.farecompare.com
- Hotels: www.hotels.com

- Hotwire: www.hotwire.com
- Kayak: www.kayak.com
- Orbitz: www.orbitz.com
- Sidestep: www.sidestep.com
- Travelocity: www.travelocity.com
- Travel Zoo: www.travelzoo.com
- Vayama: www.vayama.com
- We Go Lo: www.wegolo.com
- Yapta: www.yapta.com

Hotels for Girls' Getaway Weekends and Your Room Booking

- Hilton: www.hilton.com
- Hyatt: www.hyatt.com
- Leading Hotels of the World: www.lhw.com
- Marriottt: www.marriott.com
- Porthole (cruising website): www.porthole.com
- Radisson: www.radisson.com
- Rosewood Hotels: www.rosewoodhotels.com
- Sandals: www.sandals.com
- Sheraton: www.sheraton.com
- Westin: www.westin.com

Additional Web Sites

- Bed and Breakfast Finder: www.bnbfinder.com
- Tourism Office Worldwide Directory: www.towd.com
- Travel and Leisure Magazine (World's Best awards): www.traveland leisure.com

SHOPPING PRICE COMPARISON SITES

- www.bizrate.com
- www. dealtime.com
- www. nexttag.com
- www. pricegrabber.com

- www. shopping.com
- www. shopping.yahoo.com
- www. shopzilla.com

COUPON SOURCES

- www. coolsavings.com
- www. couponalbum.com
- www. coupongood.org
- www. coupons.com
- www. couponcabin.com
- www. couponmom.com
- www. couponmountain.com
- www. coupontweet.com
- www. dealio.com
- www. dealzconnection.com
- www. extrabux.com
- www. fabuloussavings.com
- www. fatwallet.com
- www. redtagtweets.com
- www. retailmenot.com
- www. savingpiggy.com
- www. smartsource.com
- www. ultimatecoupons.com
- www. valpak.com

Index

Acknowledgments

I must begin by thanking my amazing agent, Meredith Hays, for her enthusiasm and for her brilliant suggestions and support of this project. I'm so lucky to be in such great hands!

And many thanks to the team at Seal, starting with my editor Brooke Warner, and to Krista Lyons, Eva Zimmerman, Krissa Lagos, Christy Phillippe, and Domini Dragoone.

Big hugs to Shane McMurray at TheWeddingReport.com for granting me permission to feature his phenomenal survey results in this book.

Of course, nothing gets done around here without the love and creative inspiration I get from my amazing husband, Joe, and my brilliant bridesmaids, Jill, Jen, Pam, and Madison, who honored me by being there and by wearing those amazing Ann Taylor Celebrations sage green dresses. My girls are gorgeous!

About the Author

*S*haron Naylor is the author of over thirty-five wedding planning books, including several of the number-one-ranking brides-maid books in the country.

As a noted wedding expert and best-selling bridal author, she has appeared on top television programs including *Get Married, Good Morning America, Primetime, ABC News,* and many more. She has also been featured in *InStyle Weddings, Modern Bride, Brides, Get Married, Destination I Do, Wedding Channel, The Wall Street Journal, Bridal Guide, Southern Bride, New York Bride, New Jersey Bride,* as the resident wedding Q&A expert and spotlight blogger at iVillage, and as one of five celebrity Wedding Gurus at Weddzilla.com. She is also the host of a popular podcast on The Wedding Podcast Network, and she is a special contributor to the Bed Bath & Beyond bridal articles collection, providing advice to bridal parties and to wedding couples. Her green weddings column is featured at GorgeouslyGreen.com, as well.

She lives in Morristown, New Jersey, with her husband, Joe. Visit her website, www.sharonnaylor.net, for more information on her books and to catch her on tour to get your book signed and your bridesmaid questions answered personally.

Selected Titles from Seal Press

**For more than thirty years, Seal Press has published groundbreaking books.
By women. For women.**

Offbeat Bride: Creative Alternatives for Independent Brides, by Ariel Meadow Stallings. $16.95, 978-1-58005-315-0. Part memoir and part anecdotal how-to, *Offbeat Bride* is filled with sanity-saving tips, advice, and stories for the non-traditional bride.

Tied In Knots: Funny Stories from the Wedding Day, edited by Lisa Taggart and Samanth Schoech. $14.95, 978-1-58005-175-0. A collection of smart, original, laugh-out-loud wedding essays by women about bad luck, bad taste, and bad decisions surrounding the wedding day.

The Money Therapist: A Woman's Guide to Creating A Healthy Financial Life, by Marcia Brixey. $15.95, 978-1-58005-216-0. Offers women of every financial strata the tools they need to manage their money, set attainable budget goals, get out of debt, and create a healthy financial life.

The Choice Effect: Love and Commitment in an Age of Too Many Options, by Amalia McGibbon, Lara Vogel, and Claire A. Williams. $16.95, 978-1-58005-293-1. Three young, successful, and ambitious women provide insight into the quarterlife angst that surrounds dating and relationships and examine why more options equals less commitment for today's twentysomethings.

Just Don't Call Me Ma'am: How I Ditched the South for the Big City, Forgot My Manners, and Managed to Survive My Twenties with (Most of) My Dignity Still Intact, by Anna Mitchael. $15.95, 978-1-58005-316-7. In this disarmingly funny tale about the choices that add up to be her twentysomething life, Anna Mitchael offers young women comic relief—with the reality check that there's no possible way to hit all of their desired benchmarks on the way to thirty.

It's So You: 35 Women Write About Personal Expression Through Fashion and Style, edited by Michelle Tea. $15.95, 978-1-58005-215-3. From the haute couture houses of the ruling class to DIY girls who make restorative clothing and create their own hodgepodge style, this is the first book to explore women's ambivalence toward, suspicion of, indulgence in, and love of fashion on every level.

Find Seal Press Online
www.SealPress.com
www.facebook.com/SealPress
Twitter: @SealPress